Business Models and Innovative Technologies for SMEs

Edited By

Ignitia Motjolopane

Information Systems Department
North-West University, Mahikeng Campus,
South Africa

Ephias Ruhode

School of Business & Creative Industries
University of the West of Scotland
Glasgow, United Kingdom

&

Pius Adewale Owolawi

Faculty of Information and Communication Technology
Tshwane University of Technology
Pretoria, South Africa

Business Models and Innovative Technologies for SMEs

Editors: Ignitia Motjolopane, Ephias Ruhode & Pius Adewale Owolawi

ISBN (Online): 978-981-5196-71-9

ISBN (Print): 978-981-5196-72-6

ISBN (Paperback): 978-981-5196-73-3

Published by Bentham Science Publishers Pte. Ltd. Singapore. All Rights Reserved.

First published in 2023.

need for a court order if at any point you breach any terms of this License Agreement. In no event will any delay or failure by Bentham Science Publishers in enforcing your compliance with this License Agreement constitute a waiver of any of its rights.

3. You acknowledge that you have read this License Agreement, and agree to be bound by its terms and conditions. To the extent that any other terms and conditions presented on any website of Bentham Science Publishers conflict with, or are inconsistent with, the terms and conditions set out in this License Agreement, you acknowledge that the terms and conditions set out in this License Agreement shall prevail.

Bentham Science Publishers Pte. Ltd.
80 Robinson Road #02-00
Singapore 068898
Singapore
Email: subscriptions@benthamscience.net

BENTHAM SCIENCE

CONTENTS

PREFACE

Small and medium-sized enterprises (SMEs) are the backbone of many developing countries, contributing to economic growth and job creation. However, SMEs in these countries face a myriad of challenges that hinder their success, including limited resources, poor infrastructure, and lack of access to financing and technology. In recent years, the convergence of data analytics and artificial intelligence has presented a new set of opportunities for SMEs to navigate these challenges and unlock their potential.

Studies have shown that technologies play a major role in alleviating most of the challenges SMEs face in most developing countries. Studies also indicated that SMEs have shown remarkable resilience and adaptability in navigating the rapidly changing the business landscape. In recent years, the proliferation of disruptive technologies such as, data analytics and artificial intelligence has presented both opportunities and challenges for SMEs in developing countries. While these technologies offer new ways of doing business, SMEs often struggle to navigate the complex landscape of business models and technology adoption.

This book, titled "**Business Models and Innovative Technologies for SMEs**" aims to provide a comprehensive overview of the challenges and opportunities presented by these disruptive technologies. The book draws on the latest research and real-world case studies to offer practical insights into how SMEs can successfully navigate the changing business landscape. Drawing from real-life case studies and expert insights, the book provides a detailed analysis of the key concepts and theories related to SME business models, data analytics, and artificial intelligence, as well as their practical applications in the context of SMEs in developing countries for promoting the adoption of data-driven strategies.

The book incorporates various SME Business Models, Data Analytics, and Artificial Intelligence in the context of developing countries. It draws its use cases and insights from diverse environment academics, researchers, policymakers, and business practitioners having a core interest in SME development and the intersection of business models, data analytics, and artificial intelligence, to name a few. To be more specific, the book aims to address issues that include the following:

- What are the potential benefits of innovative technologies for SMEs?
- What is the proposed strategy model that can be used to support mobile application development for Small and Medium Enterprises (SMEs) in response to disruptive innovation?
- What are the cybersecurity risks associated with the use of modern digital technologies during the processes of digital transformation and business model innovation in Small and Medium Enterprises (SMEs), and how can appropriate cybersecurity culture be developed to protect SMEs during and after these processes?
- How can innovating SMEs' business models unleash their full innovative potential beyond simply riding on the wave of digital technology?
- How does this study contribute to the field of business model innovation, particularly in the industries that are situated in the developing countries?

The book is written based on the joint efforts of the editor, authors, and reviewers. The book mainly features qualitative, quantitative, and analytic insight into diverse case studies on SME business models, data analytics and artificial intelligence within the framework of the developing countries. The book is divided into seven chapters. This edited volume features the work of experts who bring both academic knowledge and real-world expertise to the table. Each author has made a unique contribution to this collection of writings based on their own studies and professional experiences.

The book is divided into seven chapters, each of which discusses the author's research methodologies and the context in which they were developed. The following provides a brief overview of each chapter.

Chapter 1: Business Model Innovation Mobile Application Development SMEs in Response to Disruptive Innovation

In this chapter, Dr. Francke explained Business model innovation for mobile application development for SMEs in response to disruptive innovation. This chapter proposes a multi-factorial strategy model to support mobile application development SMEs in response to disruptive innovation through business model innovation. The chapter explores the impact of artificial intelligence on various industries and suggests that SMEs in the mobile application sector should collaborate with each other to moderate their independent weaknesses. The research has developed the Disruptive Innovation State Response Model and the Disruptive Innovation Praxis Model, which can be used by development agencies, businesspersons, technologists, venture capitalists, etc. to determine the state of the business and make an appropriate response. The chapter highlights the value of the synergistic relationship of its principles.

Chapter 2: Cybersecurity Culture as a Critical Component of Digital Transformation and Business Model Innovation in SMEs

In this chapter, Prof. Zoran Mitrovic, Prof. Colin Thakur and Dr. Sudhika Palhad explain how Cybersecurity culture as a critical component of digital transformation and business model innovation in SMEs should be created in order to protect the inherent values of digital transformation. This chapter discusses how SMEs create jobs and generate tax revenue which is crucial to the economic growth of many developing countries. To keep up with the times, more and more small and medium-sized enterprises (SMEs) are adopting digital transformation (DT) and business model innovation (BMI) strategies. But if businesses do not take cybersecurity risks associated with new technology seriously, they might end up paying a high price for these inventive breakthroughs that could be disastrous. As a result, the cyber threats posed by the ICT used in DT and BMI procedures are investigated in this conceptual desktop research. It is proposed that SMEs be protected throughout and after the DT and BMI procedures by fostering a culture of adequate cybersecurity.

Chapter 3: Assessing SMEs' Business Model Innovation Readiness

In this chapter, Dr. Cecil Kgotiane carried out assessment of SME's business model innovation readiness before, during, and after the COVID-19 pandemic. This chapter titled "Assessing SMEs' business model innovation readiness", discusses two major difficulties faced by small and medium-sized enterprises (SMEs) before, during, and after the COVID-19 pandemic: their lack of preparedness to implement new business models and slow adoption of game-changing technologies like Intelligent Analytics (IA). The study focuses on a large number of SMEs in northern Gauteng, South Africa, using literature reviews, questionnaires, and on-site observations. While the study primarily focuses on Asian SMEs, the chapter concludes that the highlighted difficulties are not universal and apply to South African SMEs.

SMEs play a crucial role in society, and if they do not address these difficulties, innovation in service delivery will suffer.

The SME sector offers many possibilities for creative problem-solving, and reinventing business models is a good place to start. Simply riding the wave of digital technology may not be enough for SMEs to fully realize their potential, and they may benefit from innovating business models and adopting technologies like IA. SMEs also contribute to economic growth and need to constantly improve their strategies. Large corporations may also benefit from SMEs' novel business approaches. Improved service and product delivery have pushed society towards digitalization and disruptive technology, with IA being one such technology.

Chapter 4: Digital Transformation in SMEs: Developing Digital Business Model Innovations Based on Artificial Intelligence

In this chapter, Dr. Tlou Maggie Masenya examined the digital transformation in SMEs and developed digital business model innovations that are based on Artificial Intelligence. This chapter discusses how small and medium-sized enterprises (SMEs) are adopting modern technologies, including artificial intelligence (AI), to develop innovative business models and remain competitive in the era of digital transformation. The study reviewed literature on the impact of AI on business innovation and performance in SMEs and found that AI has the potential to revolutionize business processes, practices, and organizational performance. The article recommends that SME managers should find ways to support business innovation processes with AI and other advanced technologies to boost their dynamic capabilities, efficiency, and reduce operational risk. The major goal of every organizational strategy is to enhance the effectiveness and efficiency of operation, which could lead to organizational success. However, digital transformation presents challenges for SMEs, who need to maintain a high-performance work environment to remain competitive.

Chapter 5: Understanding the Affordances of Expert Systems in Improving the Competitiveness of South African Insurance SMEs

In this chapter, Dr. Stevens P. Mamorobela presented the role of expert systems in improving the competitiveness of South African insurance SMEs. Small and medium-sized businesses (SMEs) in South Africa's insurance market are seeking ways to improve their competitiveness. Expert systems, a newly developed technology, are expanding knowledge bases to help businesses offer insurance services more efficiently and with higher quality. However, the potential benefits of expert systems for SMEs in the insurance sector are not well understood in the literature on business model innovation. This chapter reviews the resource-based view model and proposes a model of the affordances of expert systems to help SMEs become more competitive. An explanatory mixed-method research strategy, including questionnaires and semi-structured interviews, was used to investigate the affordances of expert systems in SME insurance firms. The study found that treating the expert system as a valuable, rare, unique, low-cost, and low-risk resource can help SMEs enhance their competitiveness. This research has practical and theoretical implications for the field of business model innovation, particularly for SMEs in the insurance sector.

Chapter 6: Factors Affecting the Adoption of Data as a Service (DaaS) in Small, Medium, and Micro Enterprises (SMMEs)

In this chapter, Ms. Megan Morta and Prof. Osden Jokonya describe a research study that examined factors affecting the adoption of Data as a Service (DaaS) in Small, Medium, and Micro Enterprises (SMMEs). There have not been much research on the variables impacting the adoption of Data as a Service (DaaS) in SMMEs, despite the numerous advantages of embracing cognitive analytics, business model innovation, and data science by SMMEs. Therefore, the purpose of this chapter is to investigate what influences SMMEs to embrace Data as a Service (DaaS). The research used a comprehensive literature review to investigate what influences Small, Medium, and Micro Enterprises (SMMEs) to use DaaS. This research used the Theory of Constraints (TOC) Framework as a lens to investigate barriers to DaaS adoption in SMMEs. According to the findings, SMMEs cite technical concerns including complexity, network capacity, and availability as the most significant barriers to using DaaS. Cost, support, and infrastructure demand were also cited as the most important environmental factors influencing DaaS adoption among SMMEs. Finally, the findings show that consumer demand was deemed the most important environmental element influencing DaaS adoption in SMMEs. Finally, the study's findings indicate that technical, organizational, and environmental variables all have a role in whether or not SMMEs embrace DaaS. The research adds to the existing body of knowledge on the variables that impact the adoption of DaaS in SMMEs, notwithstanding the constraints associated with easy sampling and non-empirical data. Empirical data may be used to address the issues in future investigations.

Chapter 7: Factors Affecting the Adoption of Emerging Technologies to Reduce Food Waste by SMEs in the Food Industry

In this chapter, Ms. Talent Muzondo and Prof. Osden Jokonya confirmed that food waste is a major issue in modern society, with one-third of the world's food supply being lost or squandered every year. This study focuses on small and medium-sized enterprises (SMEs) in the food sector and what influences their adoption of new technology to reduce food waste. The research uses the TOE framework to analyze the factors that affect SMEs' likelihood to use new technology to reduce food waste. The study finds that technical criteria such as complexity, security, usability, cost, and flexibility influence SMEs' decision to adopt new technologies to decrease food waste. The size of an organization and resistance to change are significant organizational factors that influence technology adoption in the food sector. Additionally, IT policy and law are significant environmental factors influencing technology adoption. The study provides insight into the barriers that prevent SMEs in the food sector from adopting new technology to reduce food waste and highlights the need for further research.

Ignitia Motjolopane
Information Systems Department
North-West University, Mahikeng Campus,
South Africa

Ephias Ruhode
School of Business & Creative Industries
University of the West of Scotland
Glasgow, United Kingdom

&

Pius Adewale Owolawi
Faculty of Information and Communication Technology
Tshwane University of Technology
Pretoria, South Africa

List of Contributors

Colin Thakur Durban University of Technology, Berea, South Africa

Cecil Kgoetiane Department of Informatics, Faculty of ICT, Tshwane University of Technology, Pretoria, South Africa

Errol Francke Department of Information Technology, Faculty of Informatics and Design, Cape Peninsula University of Technology, Cape Town, South Africa

Megan Morta Department of Information Systems, Faculty of Economics and Management Sciences, University of the Western Cape, Cape Town, South Africa

Osden Jokonya Department of Information Systems, Faculty of Economics and Management Sciences, University of the Western Cape, Cape Town, South Africa

Sudhika Palhad Durban University of Technology, Berea, South Africa

Stevens P. Mamorobela Department of Informatics, Faculty of ICT, Tshwane University of Technology, Pretoria, South Africa

Tlou Maggie Masenya Durban University of Technology, Berea, South Africa

Talent Muzondo Department of Information Systems, Faculty of Economics and Management Sciences, University of the Western Cape, Cape Town, South Africa

Zoran Mitrovic Durban University of Technology, Berea, South Africa

CHAPTER 1

Business Model Innovation for Mobile Application Development for SMEs in Response to Disruptive Innovation

Errol Francke[1,*]

[1] *Department of Information Technology, Faculty of Informatics and Design, Cape Peninsula University of Technology, Cape Town, South Africa*

Abstract: The central proposition of this chapter is that a multi-factorial strategy model can be evolved to support mobile application development for SMEs in response to disruptive innovation through business model innovation. Artificial Intelligence is often regarded as a significantly disruptive technology impacting many industries today. AI is penetrating many sectors and transforming the tasks performed by computers. This chapter rests on two principles: the discovery of business model innovation and the type of disruption of SMEs in the mobile application sector. The fieldwork for this chapter consists of four phases. The findings and interpretations presented in this chapter imply that the rise of disruptive innovation has sparked technological advancement, which will affect SMEs in South Africa. SMEs should transition to a progressive interdependent modality where they participate using their shared strengths, according to the concept of business model innovation. They could mitigate their weaknesses by working with other mobile app development SMEs. The value of the principles' synergistic relationship has finally been revealed in the chapter. The Disruptive Innovation State Response Model and the Disruptive Innovation Praxis Model were created by this research as responses to its main thesis. A development agency, businessperson, technologist, venture capitalist, *etc.* could use these models to determine the state that the business recognizes itself in and, employing its use, generate a response that is suitable according to the chapter's final proposition.

Keywords: Artificial Intelligence, Business Model, Business Model Innovation, Commercialization, Disruptive Innovation, Disruptive Technology, Mobile Computing, Multi-Factorial Strategy Model, Praxis Model, Small Business, Strategy, Technology Innovation.

---

[*] **Corresponding author Errol Francke:** Department of Information Technology, Faculty of Informatics and Design, Cape Peninsula University of Technology, Cape Town, South Africa; Tel: 0824947851; E-mail: franckee@cput.ac.za

Ignitia Motjolopane, Ephias Ruhode and Pius Adewale Owolawi (Eds.)

INTRODUCTION

Pirola *et al*. (2020) suggested that Small and Medium Enterprises (SMEs) need to be ready for the Fourth Industrial Revolution. The authors state that SMEs are mindful of it, but management seeks ideal strategies to approach this Fourth Industrial Revolution. Along with the rise of the Fourth Industrial Revolution, Summers (2019) suggests that there are inventive prospects for SMEs to succeed using artificial intelligence (AI), which is more prolific than ever. Chonsawat & Sopadang (2021) extend the views of Pirola *et al*. (2020) by suggesting that in the Fourth Industrial Revolution, SMEs require the technology and strategy to integrate their business processes throughout. However, knowledge about technological applications in business, production, and supply chains is lacking. Rane & Narvel (2021) argue that with the rise of disruptive innovation in the Fourth Industrial Revolution, businesses should redesign their business models for these innovations to enhance agility in their operations.

Christensen *et al*. (2015) regard disruptive innovations as those upon which a product or service has been created featuring a technology originally introduced in simple applications at a lesser market price. Roblek *et al*. (2021) state that disruptive innovations "are not breakthrough innovations or ambitious upgrades" of prevailing products or services causing a shift in business models. On the contrary, they simplify and reduce the price of these products and services. In so doing, these disruptive innovations can transform the relevant industry. The transformation of these industries has been made possible by developing new business platforms that acknowledge the inefficiency of traditional organisations' pipeline architectures, which create only one income stream and have a linear value chain. Instead, industries are moving toward a model where producers, consumers, and platforms generate new connections where customers and producers exchange, consume, and jointly create value (Agyei-Boapeah, Evans & Nisar, 2022).

Khan (2022) argues that a recent technological advancement is incorporating AI into mobile applications. Existing mobile applications lack the potential to include the artificial intelligence trend, which is rapidly gaining popularity. This kind of programming has a thriving market. One of the main motives for developing applications and adding artificial intelligence to them is for top-tier mobile application development companies to upgrade their skill sets.

It is apparent that business opportunities for SMEs have emerged from the mobile application (app) market. Okonkwo & Huisman (2019) regard mobile app development as one of the most prolific technological innovations internationally. This is attributable to the rise in popularity of mobile phones and their assimilation into all aspects of society. A study conducted by Grand View Research (2020) supports the views of Okonkwo & Huisman (2019) by stating that largely because of the rise in popularity of mobile phones, coupled with the expansion of the internet and Fourth Industrial Revolution technologies, mobile apps are expected to grow in the coming years. The study states that the international mobile app market was valued at USD 154.05 billion in 2019 and is anticipated to expand at a compound annual growth rate of 11.5% from 2020 to 2027. These apps would include mobile gaming, music, health and fitness, social networking, e-commerce, *etc*.

RESEARCH PROBLEM

It appears that definite business opportunities for SMEs have arisen from the mobile app market. To ensure competitiveness and sustainability, mobile app development for SMEs needs important involvement from development agencies. The collaborative effects of disruptive innovation, business model innovation, and development agencies that support SMEs in mobile app development have received little attention in the literature. As a result, this research aims to investigate the advancement of a multi-factorial strategy model that will support the commercialisation of the mobile application development SME sector through business model innovation in response to disruptive innovation.

AIM

Based on an initial doctoral study relating to this field of research by the same author, this chapter proposes that SMEs in South Africa could exploit the potential of AI in this lucrative mobile app development market. The research aims to develop a multi-factorial strategy model to support mobile applications development for SMEs in response to disruptive innovation such as AI through business model innovation. In this chapter's perspective, a multi-factorial strategy model is considered a strategy emanating from various business inspirations describing the logic and key deliberations in establishing an SME's strategy. The management of the SME can use it to assess the company's situation and decide on the best method to innovate the business model in response to disruptive innovation.

OBJECTIVES

In striving to reach its main objective, which is to develop a multi-factorial strategy model to support mobile applications development for SMEs in response to disruptive innovation through business model innovation, this research rests on two principles:

(i) To discover the aspects of business model innovation and

(ii) To discover the type of disruption of SMEs in the mobile application sector.

LITERATURE REVIEW

An analysis of the literature suggested that the mobile app development industry might contribute significantly to the growth of the South African economy. For SMEs in this sector to benefit from the innovation in the mobile apps industry, they would need to modify their business models, especially in the wake of the Fourth Industrial Revolution, to address some of their issues. These SMEs would benefit from support and a business model innovation strategy that encourages the development of mobile apps.

At heart, the research suggested that, in response to disruptive innovation, a multi-factorial strategy model may be developed to support the SME mobile app development sector. The literature review strives to establish a cohesive outline for the fundamental ideas of the chapter. As a result, the objectives were to identify the elements of business model innovation that might contribute to the research proposition, pinpoint the relationships between the key research principles, and ultimately create a framework that links business model innovation and disruptive innovation. By developing an awareness of the existing body of knowledge, the literature review strives to advance the logic of the chapter. Considering this, the line of inquiry for this literature review would be to attempt to describe the conceptual framework within the following two principles:

i. The aspects of business model innovation, and

ii. The type of disruption.

This chapter presents a unified understanding of how the two principles work together. The main concept is a framework to support the industry regarding disruptive innovation and how it might help the development of new business models. The two concepts would be broken down into discrete understandings, and when combined, they would offer a theoretical foundation for the chapter. The chapter would primarily review business and information technology literature, but where appropriate, it would also explore outside of these fields to help clarify the two guiding concepts. The logic behind these two will be examined in detail, and a suggestion will be provided as to how these two concepts may come together.

Development of the State-response Model

This chapter's main assertion is that a multi-factorial strategy model could be developed to enable the SME sector for mobile app development in response to disruptive innovation. In this context, a multi-factorial strategy model is viewed as a method or plan that details the reasoning behind and important factors to consider while creating an organisation's strategy. SMEs can use it to assess their operations and decide on the best business model innovation to implement in response to disruptive innovation.

Through representations of parental illness, a multi-factorial model for ethnic differences in children's consultations for acute asthma was used by Sidora-Arcoleo, Feldman, Serebrisky, and Spray (2012). The authors investigated the relationships between parental representations of asthma sickness, social and environmental con,text and children's acute asthma consultations. Biological, psychological, and cultural elements, as well as their interconnections, all play a role in both health and sickness, according to a multi-factorial model put forth by Sidora-Arcoleo *et al*. (2012).

Gauthier and Lardic (2003) and Sidora-Arcoleo *et al*. (2012) also used a multi-factorial model when examining credit risks in banks. Their multi-factorial model suggests a tool for analysing and predicting credit spreads to help portfolio managers make decisions.

According to Sidora-Arcoleo *et al*. (2012) and Gauthier and Lardic (2003), similar models have been used in the social sciences and the pure sciences when a strategy had to be devised to deal with several diverse causes or influences. On how to create such a conceptual model within the social science discipline, Shoemaker *et al*. (2004) offer helpful guidance. The authors contend that creating and postulating an abstraction of reality is the process of creating a model. Modelled objects represent a system or structure; they are not exact replicas of reality but rather pure constructions of some of its most important features. A model only depicts and indicates relationships, not explains or predicts anything, as Shoemaker *et al*. (2004) point out. It can help progress theory and be a useful heuristic tool for letting users make discoveries.

Dumanski and Pieri (1995) provide their PSR model, which is utilised by organisations for environmental performance monitoring at a more practical level of model development. In their model, which is a state-response model that derives from the multi-factorial model, the authors present three conditions: first, environmental pressures brought on by human activity; second, the environment's "state," including its land, air, and water quality; and third, society's "response" to these changes through the implementation of environmental and economic programs and policies. The Dumanski and Pieri (1995) PSR approach, according to Linster (2003), emphasises cause-and-effect correlations and helps officials see the connections between environmental, economic, and other challenges (Fig. **1**).

Box 6. **Sectors in the OECD Core Set**

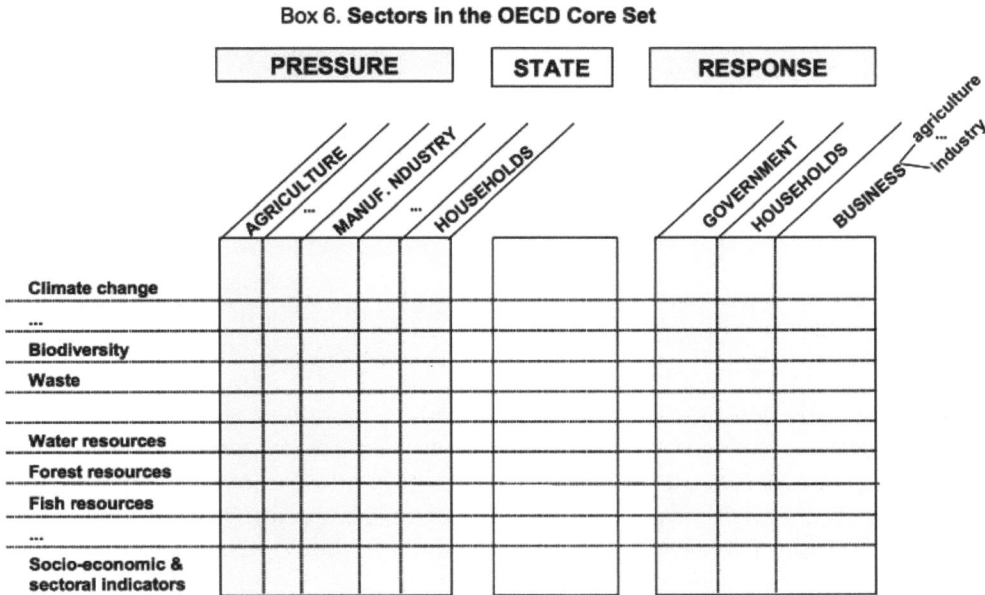

Fig. (1). Pressure–State–Response Model (Dumanski & Pieri, 1995).

In developing a Pressure-State-Response System Framework for innovation in intelligent manufacturing, Yin *et al.* (2022) argue that digital technology is an enabler in green manufacturing. The pressure-state-response (PSR) model depicts how digital technology enables the green innovation of the manufacturing industry. The authors developed a measurement system of digital green innovation in the manufacturing industry using the PSR framework.

In summary, the Pressure-State-Response indicators propose evaluating human activities' pressures on existing states and providing appropriate responses to return to a desirable state. PSR has lately been extended to social, institutional, and economic dimensions. Its value for innovation within the information communication technology context is unexplored.

The Aspects of Business Model Innovation

According to Assink (2006), Bo and Qiuyan (2012), and Kaplan (2012), the creation or reinvention of a firm itself is referred to as business model innovation (BMI). A decade later, Yi, Chen and Li (2022) extend the view of BMI by stating that it entails comprehensive changes to the organisation's boundary-spanning activity systems for producing, distributing, and capturing value. According to these definitions of BMI, changing a company's business model leads to the creation of a completely new type of enterprise that participates not only based on the value it offers in terms of its services but also based on how well it aligns its profit model, resources, and operational practices to strengthen that value proposition, capture novel market segments, and upset competitors.

New business opportunities are hampered by overemphasising product or technological innovation, which leaves a company open to attack from rivals with broad perspectives. According to Sawhney *et al.* (2006), too many companies consider innovation to be creating new products or conventional research and development. Their company suffers from this limited viewpoint since they resemble rival companies in their industry too much. To demonstrate this point, the authors highlight the capacity of Starbucks Corporation to charge higher prices for coffee than its competitors—not because their goods were any better. Starbucks Corporation successfully developed a client experience by offering a gathering place where customers could gather halfway between home and work. Considering this, the authors define business innovation as "the development of considerable new value for consumers and the firm by creatively modifying one or more characteristics of the business system" (Sawhney *et al.* 2006, p. 76). Extending the views of Sawhney *et al.* (2006), Palmié, Miehé, Oghazi, Parida, and Wincent (2022) suggest the rapid advancement of digital technologies and the data they produce are altering the nature of competition in several different businesses. These advancements show how digital technologies give rise to numerous new avenues for value creation, which greatly impact business models.

These authors support the idea that SMEs should concentrate on the entire business system and the value they provide to their clients rather than just on product or technology innovation. This chapter suggests that there are many ways in which business innovation can be described. Business innovation is about creating new value rather than just new products since innovation is only important if it benefits customers and if they are willing to pay for it. Additionally, innovation can take various forms because it can occur in any aspect of a business, such as altering client segments, consumer products, or process improvement. Finally, since business innovation is systemic, it necessitates a thorough study of every business area.

Åström, Reim & Parida (2022) state that the development of AI technology opens up new possibilities for businesses to give value to their consumers by taking a proactive approach, managing uncertainty, and boosting cost-effectiveness and revenue. However, AI technology's capabilities alone are insufficient; businesses also need to comprehend how the technology can be made commercially viable through inventive AI business models. Business-model ideas frequently need to be drastically changed when new technology is introduced. This is essential to fully benefit from disruptive technologies since creating cutting-edge technology solutions is just as crucial as innovating the business strategy. Mueller (2022) suggests that companies must consider changes in products and processes more than changes in technology if digital transformation is to be meaningful and long-lasting. But many businesses find it difficult to see through the alluring claims that frequently accompany new technologies. As a result, they focus too much of their attention and resources on the technological aspect of digital transformation initiatives. Thinking about digitalisation as a business model innovation rather than a change in technology is one way to address this imbalance.

The body of knowledge contains many definitions of business models. In light of the aforementioned points concerning business models, DaSilva and Trkman's (2014) present a thesis that when a business fails, it is frequently criticised even if it would be more proper to criticize how it is executed is relevant to this chapter. Porter (1990) also warns against the risk that separating the business model from the company's strategy could undermine the firm's key competitive advantages. According to the author, a company must continue to innovate because it is continually exposed to new rivals and inferior products. Of significance to this chapter is the contribution of Åström, Reim & Parida (202,2), who recommend that it is important to clarify how businesses exploring the potential of AI link value-creation and value-capture aspects to create AI business models that are both profitable and scalable.

The Type of Disruptive Innovation

After reflecting on the opinions of Christensen *et al.* (2015), Rane & Narvel (2021), Roblek *et al.* (2021) and Khan (2022), this chapter defines disruptive innovation as an innovation that initially aids in the development of a new market and value network before disrupting an existing market and value network (over years or decades) and replacing an earlier technology.

The body of knowledge suggests that disruptive innovation is an innovation that affects fundamental changes in many industries and operates at a business and technology level. This is supported by Christensen *et al.* (2015) and Bashir *et al.* (2016), who contend that disruptive innovation focuses on business models, processes, revenue streams, market dynamics, and customer behaviour in addition to technology innovation. Of significance to this chapter is to question the fundamental or inherent characteristics, origins, and traits of the innovation in the quest to comprehend the nature of disruptive innovation.

Agyei-Boapeah, Evans & Nisar (2022) propose that advances in information and communication technologies (ICTs), cultural norms, and economic realities involve businesses establishing new types of possibilities and competition through the exploitation of business platforms—have all contributed to the proliferation of disruptive innovation. Established service sectors like hospitality, transportation, and financial services have been significantly impacted by disruptive innovation by eliminating 'middlemen,'. These new emerging structures connect various services and goods providers with various customer types, creating and transferring value between markets.

The Business Value of Artificial Intelligence

Otar (2019) states that one of the most disruptive contemporary technologies is proving to be AI. Businesses worldwide use it in several ways, from establishing product/market fit to automating customer conversations. Small businesses can assess client feedback from communication channels with the aid of AI and then automatically change their lead generation and marketing strategies in response to that data. AI technologies have been created that can speed up the hiring and onboarding process and gather feedback from new hires on how human resources can make those procedures even more efficient. Both improvements can significantly affect a business's bottom line.

Mills (2019) argues that technology, specifically artificial intelligence, can help small businesses as they are already transforming the corporate world, and they appear to be benefiting big businesses thus far. The key question is whether they can be created and used to support smaller enterprises and large corporations.

McRorey (2021) extends the views of Otar (2019) by suggesting that the business world is discovering that AI has the power to automate its processes rather than execute every task by hand. AI leads them to generate higher productivity, fewer mistakes, and ultimately higher revenues. Even if there are numerous AI solutions on the market right now, not all of them will necessarily be fit for purpose. A chatbot is a popular simple option that many small businesses have opted to use as their initial point of contact when responding to customers online. This simple-t--implement approach can connect the social media accounts of a business and, in so doing, boost its chances of gaining more devoted customers. McRorey (2021) warns that understanding all important business data points and stakeholders' readiness to support the initiative are caveats. It will necessitate a long-term commitment, both to the initiative and the security procedures required to safeguard the data of the business and its clients.

Valcheva (2022) states that AI is not just for major corporations and international IT giants. Every forward-thinking small business that wants to expand and stay one step ahead of the competition needs AI. The business goals will determine the specifics of how it will use AI. How the business is managed could change, enabling smarter decisions to be made more rapidly. The AI landscape will change the standards by which businesses will compete. It will present a tremendous opportunity for businesses with a forward-thinking attitude.

Summary of the Literature

In essence and key to the focus of this chapter, then, are the views of Valcheva (2022) which suggests that there is a need for small businesses to consider business model innovation to take advantage of the benefits that AI could bring to small businesses. Of further significance would be how SMEs in the mobile app development sector could benefit from AI by innovating their business models accordingly. Identifying how such ICT developments will impact business models and the significance of companies acting effectively using innovation is the business problem.

The literature barely scratches the surface of the fact that the dimension of business model innovation is (1) the creation of substantial new value for customers and the company, (2) ongoing surveillance of new competitors and substitute products, and (3) attaining business viability and an ongoing competitive advantage. Business model innovation appears to have the potential to lead to business growth and opportunity. Business model innovation refers to the development or revision of a business model. The literature claims that business owners underuse the prospect of business model innovation to modify their current businesses, which harms their expansion and sustainability.

In light of the research's current state, various authors have advanced various aspects of disruptive innovation. Disruptive innovation capability is crucial for business expansion and market preservation, according to the literature. Disruptive innovation demands that leaders and the organizations that train them adopt new mindsets and behaviours. The body of literature seems to concur that disruptive innovation is an innovation that brings about a significant shift in how sectors function, is problematic and unpredictable, and is dynamic. Innovation takes place not only at the technological level but also at the SME business level.

METHODOLOGY

A business network is formed by the interaction of organisations and how they function as a unit, sustaining and transforming one another. Based on this, the Critical Realism approach was found to help describe the construct of business model innovation because it reflects its dynamic interactional nature in terms of ontology (view of the nature of reality), epistemology (view of the nature of knowledge), and methodology (view of the appropriate ways to study knowledge). The methodology is founded on the basic principles of Critical Realism, namely the existence of a structured real world, the fact that knowledge is socially produced, and the pursuit of the generative mechanisms that help us understand empirical experiences.

This chapter used an inductive approach, so observations and interpretations on various topics or experiences could be generated. The fieldwork involved four stages of data collection processes. A purposive (judgmental) sampling technique was employed that chose participants purposefully due to their qualities.

Stage One

In-depth interviews were conducted with SMEs in the vicinity of Cape Town that develop mobile apps and software. The purpose was to map out the Western Cape's mobile applications development market. This was accomplished using a structured survey tool that included telephone and in-person engagement. The sample size of seven was limited by the businesses' willingness to participate in interviews. The findings were interpreted qualitatively rather than quantitatively due to the very small sample size of respondents, where the validity and trustworthiness of the data could be questioned.

Stage Two

A focused interview was conducted with a representative from business development agencies and a mobile app development industry representative. The specific goal was to test the results of stage one of the empirical work and to triangulate these results with those from the literature review. The intention was an attempt to describe the aspects of business model innovation and the type of disruption impacting this sector.

Stage Three

In stage three, interviews were conducted with entrepreneurs in the innovation and technology sector. This involved interviewing 10 additional SMEs in the innovation and technology sector based on the responses from the focused interview in stage three. Interview transcripts were analysed after being recorded. The results of this round of interviews were triangulated with the results of stage 2.

Stage Four

Finally, stage four included interviews with 12 business development agencies that support the development of SMEs. The interviews incorporated the synopsis of stages one to four and were recorded, and the transcripts were analysed.

An adaptation of the Delphi research method was used to improve the validity and credibility of the findings. First, a focused interview was conducted between business representatives and the development agency. This interview aimed to learn more about the innovation and technology sector, analyse it, and generate some assumptions. The subsequent step featured several data collection and analysis techniques used in an iterative process to gather and filter the opinions, first of industry experts. Following data analysis, the second round of interviews— based on the initial round of interviews with industry representatives—was conducted with development agencies. The multi-factorial strategy model was then enhanced with the combined feedback from the business sector and development agencies.

RESULTS

Stage One

Four of the seven companies had previously worked on mobile application development projects. Three of these companies created their apps with customers in mind and want to make money from them. After successfully completing their apps, the two companies could not profit from them. Commercialisation is a difficult task. Most of these companies hire outside companies to handle one or more tasks related to developing mobile applications. The design of the application is an example of a typical outsourced task.

Stage Two

Understanding the nature of disruptive innovation is crucial, and it is critical to comprehend how industry experts and development agencies define the characteristics of business model innovation. Everyone agrees that innovation among South African companies must improve from technology adoption to real innovation. The means to do so must be explored.

The development agency has a crucial role in promoting the sustainability of SMEs in this industry. Because a strong emphasis on research and development is crucial for the sustainability of the entrepreneur, higher education institutions should also recognise their significance as a development agency in the innovation arena.

Understanding the main constructs is crucial when analysing the mobile app development ecosystem. Businesses in South Africa are followers, benchmarking to a minimal level of international conformity. As a result, these companies are more technology implementers than true innovators. All of the technologies are being used by the role players. They don't care about international borders and are prepared to conduct business on a continental scale if necessary. They are primarily playing for financial gain but also considering their own needs and interests.

Stage Three

100% of the SMEs agreed that a business must be responsive to unpredictable and disruptive market forces.

90% agreed that a business must turn an innovation into a business that can succeed and ensure its long-term sustainability.

90% agreed that it is crucial for a business to take a new technological solution from a real or perceived need and to develop this technology into a viable entity by introducing it to the market.

90% agreed that a business must have a proactive approach to the marketplace when it believes market interest in its offering may be low or dwindling.

80% agreed that a business must pursue the research and development of new products to ensure its sustainability.

100% agreed that a business must interrogate how it conducts it to enhance its service offering.

The assistance that SMEs in this industry need from the development agency is represented by the prevailing themes listed below:

I. Strategic Support

II. Capacity Building

III. Promotion of Opportunity

IV. Growth and Sustainability

V. Collaboration (a nascent theme)

Stage Four

The development agencies found the following elements in characterising how SMEs in this area go about running their businesses:

I. Static Business Model: The SMEs approach product and service development, as well as business in general, rigidly and sequentially. This linear strategy makes it challenging for organisations to adapt swiftly to change.

II. Venture Participation: It appears that the SMEs are taking part in the course of action based on accepted and normative practices.

III. Technology Acquisition: Rather than creating these technologies internally the SMEs are acquiring them from their industry.

IV. Market Access & Penetration: The SMEs seem to be able to access their existing clientele, and in a certain market, existing clients are aware of and purchase their goods or services.

V. Product Adaptation: Rather than creating game-changing breakthroughs, the various goods offered by the SMEs seem to have developed through minor alterations or improvements to those of their competitors or current products.

VI. Service Adaptation: It appears that the SMEs run operations that imitate the services they provide to customers based on industry standards set by their rivals and suppliers.

The development agencies classified the help needed from SMEs in this industry into the following categories:

I. Agile Business Model

II. Venture Creation

III. Technology Innovation

IV. Market Creation

V. Product Innovation

VI. Service Innovation

Summary of the Results

The application development companies recognised the potential of mobile applications, but they appeared to be having difficulty commercialising these apps. The SMEs agreed that being responsive to unpredictable and disruptive market forces was critical for a business. A company must turn an innovation into a successful business and thus ensure its long-term viability. A business needs to take a new technological solution that arises from a real or perceived need and turn it into a viable entity by introducing it to the market. When SMEs believe that market interest in their offering is low or dwindling, they must take a proactive approach to the market. They all affirmed that a company needed to pursue research and development of new products to ensure its long-term viability. Finally, the SMEs accepted that a company must question how it conducts business to improve its service offering.

The following dominant themes represent the assistance of SMEs in this sector, namely, Strategic Support, Capacity Building, Promotion of Opportunity and Growth, and Sustainability.

The findings indicate that more research is needed to develop a model that can provide a strategy for enhanced commercialisation of mobile application development to assist businesses in mobile application development. Depending on the business's propensity for mobile application development, this model must address several issues. It is also recommended to research what changes to these businesses' current business models are required to enter into mobile application development.

ANALYSIS

Despite the potential of mobile applications, Western Cape-based firms that build them have difficulty turning a profit. More research is needed to establish a multi-factorial strategy model that could improve the commercialisation of mobile app development. This strategy must address several problems, depending on the company's choice for creating mobile apps. Research on the adjustments these companies' current business models must make to accommodate mobile app development was also encouraged.

The results and interpretations of this research indicated a structured real world of the mobile apps development industry in the Western Cape, South Africa, by identifying its main constructs. It was then revealed that knowledge is socially produced by establishing the key imperatives guiding the development agent's involvement in business models and disruptive innovation. The emancipated agenda of mobile application development in the Western Cape, South Africa, was exposed through critical discourse analysis of the respondents' opinions. In the end, this process revealed the generative mechanisms that help us understand, among other things, what the fundamental performance underpinnings are.

To counter disruptive innovation, which is described as "new technology whose entry into the market signals the inevitable displacement of the dominant technology in that sector," it is advised that the SME sector employ business model innovation (Ganguly, Nilchiani & Farr, 2010, p. 35). Disruptive innovation has given rise to technical innovation, which will influence SMEs in South Africa. SMEs should transition to a progressive interdependent modality where they engage using their shared strengths, according to the concept of business model innovation. Their flaws could be mitigated by working with other mobile app development SMEs. Mobile app development SMEs should be able to respond to disruptive innovation and assure success and sustainability through business model innovation. Progressive management through business model innovation should be the cure for disruption. In this regard, the solution to disruptive innovation is a management reaction that should be comprehended throughout the sector in which the research is conducted.

Disruptive Innovation State Response Model

The idea of technology transfer and commercialisation is crucial to this chapter. According to the research, a multi-factorial strategy model could be created to enable development agencies to increase the commercialisation of the SME sector for developing mobile apps through developing new business models in response to disruptive innovation. A specific multi-factorial strategy model was created for this research based on the validation of the usefulness of models from Dumanski and Pieri (1995), Gauthier and Lardic (2003), Linster (2003), Shoemaker *et al.* (2004), and Sidora-Arcoleo *et al.* (2012).

The Disruptive Innovation State Response Model, shown in Fig. (**2**), is the final manifestation of this multi-factorial strategy model.

Disruptive Innovation State Response Model

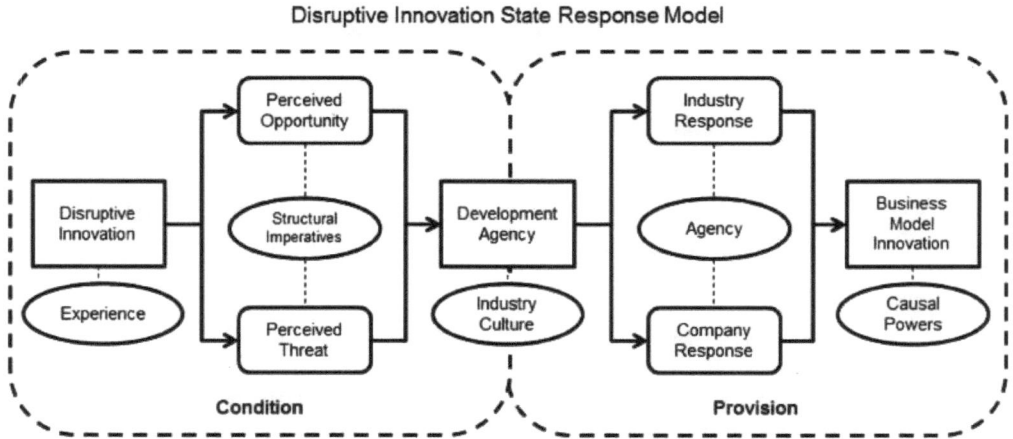

Fig. (2). The Disruptive Innovation State Response Model.

Disruptive Innovation Praxis Model

The relationship between the state of the disruptive innovation and the response of the business model innovation within the actual business ecosystem is depicted in the Disruptive Innovation State Response Model. Still, it is simplified and more applicable in the Disruptive Innovation Praxis Model. Disruptive innovation typically emerges in low-end or emerging markets, enabling smaller companies with limited resources to compete successfully against established incumbents. Additionally, it may influence businesses at different organisational, technological, or sectoral levels. Regardless of the disruptive innovation's nature, the business is in a specific situation within the market, and the response to the disruptive innovation needs to be appropriate for that situation.

Two axes make up the praxis model. The first is the condition for disruptive innovation. These are features, functions, goods or services, and technological platforms. Although these ideas already exist, they were never developed according to the disruptive innovation condition paradigm. They are an abductive interpretation of the literature on data interviews that serves as a thematic definition of the disruptive innovation condition. These were not just thematic conditions but also manifested in the feature, function, product/service, and technological platform hierarchical sequence shown in Fig. (3).

Disruptive Innovation Praxis Model

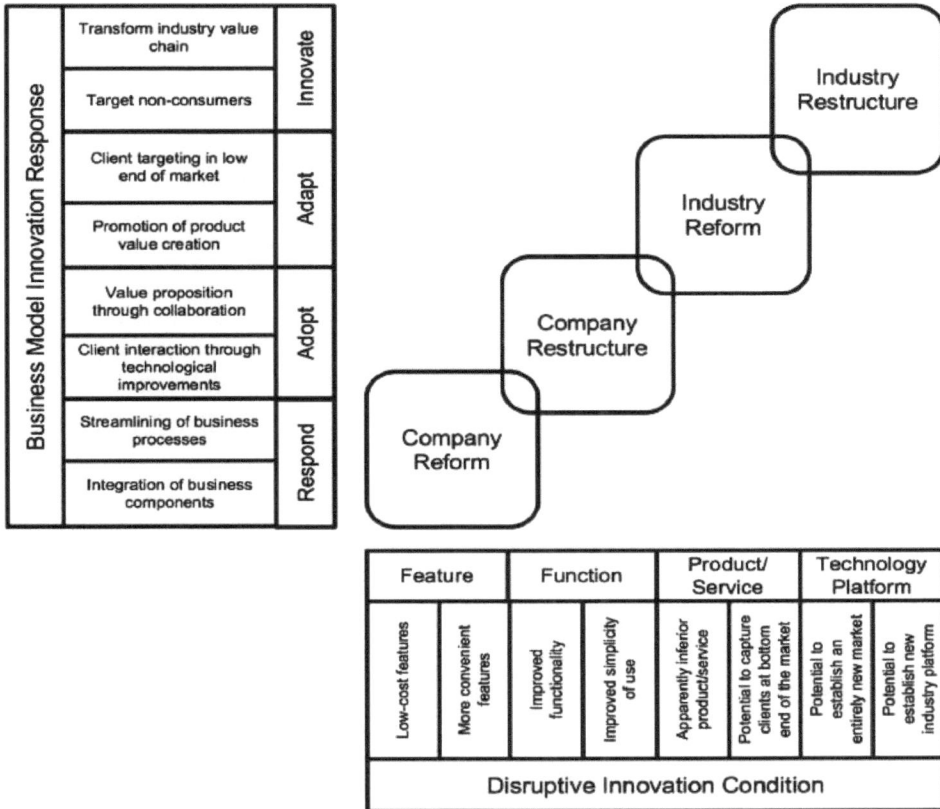

Fig. (3). The Disruptive Innovation Praxis Model.

Like this, the business model innovation response must respond, adopt, adapt, and innovate in relation to the disruptive innovation situation. Though not particularly novel ideas, these have been made clear by retroductive reasoning. Abductive reasoning is used to arrive at the linear hierarchy of the business model innovation response, accept, adapt, and innovate. The performance paradigm is presented by company reform, company restructure, industry reform, and industry restructure. It is suggestive rather than decisive because it is entirely inductive. For instance, if a function leads to adoption, it necessitates company restructuring, as shown in Fig. (3).

CONCLUSION

AI is more accessible than ever, and there are creative options for small businesses to prosper with it. Businesses now have new opportunities to enhance customer experiences, supplement staffing, and expedite their operational procedures thanks to advanced AI solutions that are more easily and affordably available than before.

The significance of this socio-technical research resides in how well it responds to its primary research question: "How can a multi-factorial strategy model be established to help mobile application development SMEs respond to disruptive innovation through business model innovation?"

The chapter tries to explain and analyse, rather than merely describe, the SME world's structure, culture, and agency in this sector. Finding the synergistic interaction between the two concepts will reveal the answer to the main research question. Progressive management using new business models must be the remedy for disruption. Therefore, a management response is an antidote to disruptive innovation, but everyone in the sector where the research is being conducted must understand this. What is expected of management is that it must create a paradigm shift in how the idea of a firm is transformed overall. This opinion is supported by the knowledge that disruptive innovation necessitates a disruptive approach to management and is likely more about best principles than best practices (Kaplan, 2012).

The chapter explicitly suggests that SMEs could employ a particular multi-factorial strategy model, known as the Disruptive Innovation State Response Model, to respond to disruptive innovation. A more streamlined depiction of the interaction between the state of the disruptive innovation and the response of the business model innovation within the actual firm is provided by the Disruptive Innovation Praxis Model. The opinions and suggestions of Dumanski and Pieri (1995), Gauthier and Lardic (2003), Linster (2003), Shoemaker *et al.* (2004), and Sidora-Arcoleo *et al.* served as a guide for the creation of these models (2012).

The scope of this research exposed some shortcomings while also providing prospects for further investigation. These restrictions may be connected to the type or scope of empirical studies. The special nature of empirical research methods could constrain the generalizability of the findings. Before extrapolating the findings beyond the specific categories of SMEs that took part in the survey, this should be considered. Most of the SMEs were black-owned and managed by males in the formal economy based in the Cape Metropole, which could lead to sample bias. Since responses from SMEs in the expanded Western Cape and rural areas can differ from those of the existing respondents, there may be a possible non-response bias. Therefore, future research should have a larger, more geographically diverse sample of SMEs to show the generalisability of the outcomes of this chapter. Future research may also focus on applying the Condition-Provision Model, a key component of the Disruptive Innovation State Response Model, to industries other than technology.

This chapter's importance ultimately rests on its contribution to the debate on SME performance, which benefits the SA economy. The value proposition of the research, according to its conclusion, is that a development agency, businessperson, technologist, venture capitalist, *etc.*, could use the Disruptive Innovation State Response Model and the Disruptive Innovation Praxis Model to identify the paradigm that the business is currently operating in and, through its application, respond appropriately.

GLOSSARY

Artificial Intelligence	Artificial intelligence (AI) is a branch of computer science that deals with creating intelligent agents which are systems that can reason, learn, and act autonomously.
Business Model	A business model describes how a company creates delivers, and captures value. It is a blueprint for how the company will make money.
Business Model Innovation	Business model innovation is the process of creating new or significantly changing existing business models. It is a way for companies to create new sources of value or to improve their competitive position.
Commercialization	Commercialization is the process of bringing a new product or service to market. It involves several steps including product development, market research, and sales and marketing.
Disruptive Innovation	Disruptive innovation is a term to describe a new product or service that displaces an existing one. Disruptive innovations are often cheaper simpler, or more convenient than existing products or services, and they can often appeal to new markets.
Disruptive Technology	Disruptive technology is a type of technology that has the potential to significantly change the way we live and work. Disruptive technologies are often characterised by their low cost ease of use, and scalability.
Innovation.	Innovation is the process of creating new or improved products services, or processes. Innovation is essential for companies that want to be successful in the long term.
Mobile Computing	Mobile computing is the use of portable devices such as smartphones and tablets, to access the internet and other computing resources. Mobile computing has become increasingly popular in recent years, as devices have become more powerful and affordable.
Multi-Factorial Strategy Model	The multi-factorial strategy model is a business strategy framework that identifies key factors that contribute to business success. It is a valuable tool for companies wanting sustainable competitive advantage.

Praxis Model	The praxis model is a framework for understanding and improving organisational performance. It emphasises the importance of taking action and experimenting to learn and grow.
Small Business	A small business is a business that is independently owned and operated. Small businesses play an important role in the economy providing jobs and innovation.
Strategy	Strategy is the process of making choices about how to achieve a desired outcome. A good strategy is based on a clear understanding of the environment the company's strengths and weaknesses, and the company's goals.
Technology	Technology is the application of scientific knowledge to practical problems. Technology can be used to improve the way we live and work.

REFERENCES

Agyei-Boapeah, H, Evans, R & Nisar, TM (2022) Disruptive innovation: Designing business platforms for new financial services. *J Bus Res,* 150, 134-46.
[http://dx.doi.org/10.1016/j.jbusres.2022.05.066]

Assink, M (2006) Inhibitors of disruptive innovation capability: A conceptual model. *Eur J Innov Manage,* 9, 215-33.
[http://dx.doi.org/10.1108/14601060610663587]

Åström, J, Reim, W & Parida, V (2022) Value creation and value capture for AI business model innovation: A three-phase process framework. *Rev Manag Sci,* 16, 2111-33.

Bo, Z & Qiuyan, T (2012) Research of SMEs' technology innovation model from multiple perspectives. *Chi Manag Stud,* 6, 124-36.
[http://dx.doi.org/10.1108/17506141211213825]

Chonsawat, N & Sopadang, A (2021) Smart SMEs 4.0 Maturity Model to Evaluate the Readiness of SMEs Implementing Industry 4.0. *CMUJ. Nat. Sci.* 20(2), e2021027.

Christensen, CM, Raynor, ME & McDonald, R (2015) What is disruptive innovation? *Harv Bus Rev,* 93, 44-53.
[PMID: 17183796]

DaSilva, CM & Trkman, P (2014) Business model: What it is and what it is not. *Long Range Plann,* 47, 379-89.
[http://dx.doi.org/10.1016/j.lrp.2013.08.004]

Dumanski, J & Pieri, C (1995) *Application of the pressure-state-response framework for the land quality indicators (LQI) programme.*Food and Agriculture Organization of the United Nations, Rome. http://www.fao.org/docrep/w4745e/w4745e08.htm

Ganguly, A, Nilchiani, R & Farr, JV (2010) Defining a set of metrics to evaluate the potential disruptiveness of a technology. *Eng Manag J,* 22, 34-44.
[http://dx.doi.org/10.1080/10429247.2010.11431851]

Gauthier, C & Lardic, S (2003) Un modèle multifactoriel des spreads de crédit : Estimation sur panels complets et incomplets. *Économie & prévision,* 159, 53-69. [A multifactorial model of credit spreads: an estimation using complete and incomplete panels].
[http://dx.doi.org/10.3917/ecop.159.0053]

Grand View Research (2020) *Healthcare Mobile Application Market Size, Share & Trends Analysis Report By Type (Fitness Products Training, Appointment Booking & Construction), By Platform, By Technology, By End User, And Segment Forecasts.* 2020 – 2027. Available from: https://www.grandviewresearch.com/industry-analysis/healthcare-mobile-applications-market

Kaplan, S (2012) Leading disruptive innovation. Available from: iveybusinessjournal.com/

publication/leading-disruptive-innovation/

Khan, W (2022) *How To Use Artificial Intelligence in Mobile Apps.* Available from: https://elearningindustry.com/how-to-use-artificial-intelligence-in-mobile-apps (Accessed on 21 June 2022).

Linster, M (2003) *OECD environmental indicators: Development, measurement and use.* OECD, Paris. Available from: https://www.oecd.org/env/indicators-modelling-outlooks/24993546.pdf (Accessed on 10 January 2017).

McRorey, L (2021) *Five ways ai can take small businesses to the next level.* Available from: https://www.forbes.com/sites/forbestechcouncil/2021/06/10/five-ways-ai-can-take--mall-businesses-to-the-next-level/?sh=6e2b85ec7a53 (Accessed on 22 June 2022).

Mills, K (2019) How AI Could help small businesses', entrepreneurship, harvard business review. Available from: https://hbr.org/2019/06/how-ai-could-help-small-businesses (Accessed on 21 June 2022).

Mueller, B (2022) *How to Map Out Your Digital Transformation.* Available from: https://hbr.org/2022/04/how-to-map-out-your-digital-transformation (Accessed on 22 June 2022).

Okonkwo, C & Huisman, M (2019) The predicting success factors of mobile applications development: Organizational perspectives. *12ʰ IADIS International Conference Information Systems.*

Otar, C (2019) Four ways artificial intelligence can help your small business, forbes finance council. Available from: https://www.forbes.com/sites/forbesfinancecouncil/2019/04/09/four-ways-artifici-l-intelligence-can-help-your-small-business/?sh=790038434a1a (Accessed on 23 June 2022).

Palmié, M, Miehé, L, Oghazi, P, Parida, V & Wincent, J (2022) The evolution of the digital service ecosystem and digital business model innovation in retail: The emergence of meta-ecosystems and the value of physical interactions. *Technol Forecast Soc Change, 177,* 121496. [http://dx.doi.org/10.1016/j.techfore.2022.121496]

Pirola, F, Cimini, C & Pinto, R (2019) Digital readiness assessment of Italian SMEs: A case-study research. *J Manuf Tech Manag, 31,* 1045-83. [http://dx.doi.org/10.1108/JMTM-09-2018-0305]

Porter, ME (1990) *The competitive advantage of nations.* Free Press, New York, NY. [http://dx.doi.org/10.1007/978-1-349-11336-1]

Rane, SB & Narvel, YAM (2021) Re-designing the business organization using disruptive innovations based on blockchain-IoT integrated architecture for improving agility in future Industry 4.0. *Benchmarking, 28,* 1883-908. [http://dx.doi.org/10.1108/BIJ-12-2018-0445]

Roblek, V, Meško, M, Pušavec, F & Likar, B (2021) The role and meaning of the digital transformation as a disruptive innovation on small and medium manufacturing enterprises. *Front Psychol, 12,* 592528. [http://dx.doi.org/10.3389/fpsyg.2021.592528] [PMID: 34177680]

Sawhney, M, Wolcott, RC & Arroniz, I (2006) The 12 different ways for companies to innovate. *MIT Sloan Manag Rev, 47,* 75-81.

Shoemaker, PJ, Tankard, JW & Lasorsa, DL (2004) *How to build social science theories.* Sage, Thousand Oaks, CA. [http://dx.doi.org/10.4135/9781412990110]

Sidora-Arcoleo, K, Feldman, JM, Serebrisky, D & Spray, A (2012) A multi-factorial model for examining racial and ethnic disparities in acute asthma visits by children. *Ann Behav Med, 43,* 15-28. [http://dx.doi.org/10.1007/s12160-011-9328-3] [PMID: 22160799]

Summers, B (2019) *How Artificial Intelligence Services Can Help Small Businesses.* Available from: https://www.forbes.com/sites/forbesbusinesscouncil/2022/01/19/how-artificial-intelligence-servi-es-can-help-small-businesses/?sh=2d9f14997393

Valcheva, S (2022) *10 Ways Artificial Intelligence Helps Business: Uses & Examples.* Available from: https://www.intellspot.com/artificial-intelligence-business/

Yi, Y, Chen, Y & Li, D (2022) Stakeholder ties, organizational learning, and business model innovation: A business ecosystem perspective. *Technovation,* 114, 102445.
[http://dx.doi.org/10.1016/j.technovation.2021.102445]

Yin, S, Zhang, N, Ullah, K & Gao, S (2022) Enhancing digital innovation for the sustainable transformation of manufacturing industry: A pressure-state-response system framework to perceptions of digital green innovation and its performance for green and intelligent manufacturing. *Systems,* 10, 72.
[http://dx.doi.org/10.3390/systems10030072]

Cybersecurity Culture as a Critical Component of Digital Transformation and Business Model Innovation in SMEs

Zoran Mitrovic[1,*], **Colin Thakur**[1] and **Sudhika Palhad**[1]

[1] Durban University of Technology, Berea, South Africa

Abstract: Small and medium enterprises (SMEs) are crucial to national and regional development and are significant drivers of job creation and income generation. To remain competitive, SMEs are increasingly adopting Digital Transformation (DT) and Business Model Innovation (BMI) to take advantage of modern digital technologies. However, these transformations can also pose serious cybersecurity risks if organisations do not prioritise cybersecurity threats associated with these modern technologies. Therefore, this conceptual desktop study examines the cybersecurity risks of information and communication technologies (ICT) utilised in DT and BMI processes and recommends fostering an appropriate cybersecurity culture to protect SMEs during and after these transformations.

Keywords: Business model innovation (BMI), Cybersecurity culture, Digital transformation (DT), Small and medium enterprises (SMEs).

INTRODUCTION

Small and medium enterprises (SMEs) are viewed as key drivers of both national and regional development in numerous countries and play a crucial role in generating employment opportunities and income (Demirguc-Kunt, 2007). Hence, they are seen as significant contributors to economic development (OECD, 2014). In South Africa, the country where the authors come from, SMEs contribute significantly to the economy, roughly 34% of South Africa's Gross Domestic Product (GDP) and play a vital role as drivers for reducing unemployment. Also, SMEs employ about 60% of the workforce in South Africa (IFC, 2021). However, South Africa is no exception as many developing economies are pursuing their growth by stabilising their SME sector (Masroor & Asim, 2019).

[*] **Corresponding author Zoran Mitrovic:** Durban University of Technology, Berea, South Africa; Tel: +27 31 373 6473; E-mail: ZoranM@dut.ac.za

Ignitia Motjolopane, Ephias Ruhode and Pius Adewale Owolawi (Eds.)

Conversely, it is widely believed that SMEs are susceptible to a variety of social, economic, technological, cultural, environmental, and management-related factors that make them vulnerable. These challenges are viewed as competitive factors that contribute to the shorter lifespan and failure of SMEs (Prasanna *et al.*, 2019). Thus, SMEs are advised to adopt information and communication technologies (ICT) as a way to address the competitive challenges they face (Nugroho *et al.*, 2017). Embracing ICT leads to lower operational costs, better customer service, and enhanced responsiveness between SMEs, their customers, and suppliers. In addition, it enhances market intelligence and strengthens the relationship with trading partners. These benefits are the reason for the adoption of ICT by SMEs (Prasanna *et al*, 2019).

It is now well known that modern societies are driven by all-perversive ICT. The ongoing trend in digitalisation is continually transforming the business world and our society. There has been an ongoing discussion regarding how businesses of all sizes can incorporate new technologies into their innovation models to generate value. This trend of heavily relying on modern ICT to enhance business processes is referred to as Digital Transformation (DT) (Legner *et al.* 2017). Moreover, to keep up with technological advancements and the societal changes brought on by generations X, Y, and Z, businesses must address these challenges with innovative solutions and the use of various modern technologies. This is an essential practice for businesses to adopt if they aim to thrive in a global market that is continuously disrupted by rapid and unpredictable changes, where the modern customer is a collaborator in value creation (Ziółkowska, 2021).

However, DT frequently triggers significant transformations that take place at various levels, shaping how agents innovate by identifying, grasping, and modifying opportunities created by the new digital paradigm across all types of organisations (Appio *et al.*, 2020). The potential disruptive impact of digital transformation on innovation and Business Model Innovation (BMI) is apparent (Bughin, 2017; Cozzolino *et al.*, 2018). For instance, well-known digital innovations such as Uber, Airbnb, and Spotify challenge the existence of established companies and create significant systemic effects in markets and industries (Skog *et al.*, 2018). Hence, to stay competitive, SMEs must innovate, changing themselves, amongst others, through innovating their business models.

However, many South African SMEs are yet to introduce appropriate digital transformation strategies and processes in their organisation. The research findings suggest that SMEs in South Africa have only adopted a limited number of digital transformation strategies, such as online selling, social media marketing, and web design. Other effective digital marketing techniques such as application development, video production, email marketing, search engine optimization and marketing, branding, and content marketing are yet to be embraced by SMEs. According to Jeza and Lekhanya (2022), these marketing techniques have the potential to significantly expand the reach of SMEs and contribute to their growth.

To fully leverage the advantages of DT and BMI, it is crucial to prioritise the secure utilisation of modern ICT. Additionally, SMEs must effectively handle cyber risks as they transition to the digital realm and adopt new digital solutions (Huzaizi *et al.*, 2021). Furthermore, SMEs will need to properly manage cyber risks as they connect to the digital world and progress towards new digital solutions (Huzaizi *et al.*, 2021). The need for cybersecurity should not hinder anyone from engaging in business activities online (Ghernaouti & Wanner, 2018). This primarily requires capacitating humans as they are still the weakest link in cybersecurity (De Maggio *et al.*, 2019). Extant literature suggests that a significant number of cyberattacks arise from people's non-compliant behaviour (Njoroge, 2020).

Since people can pose a threat and vulnerability to a company's informational resources, individuals need to take responsibility for promoting a secure and watchful culture at work (Ismail & Yusof, 2018). The evidence strongly indicates that developing and sustaining a culture of cybersecurity is crucial. This is because such a practice is increasingly acknowledged as an efficient way of addressing human factors in various types of organisations (ENISA, 2018). This highlights the need to promote a cybersecurity culture (Reegård *et al.*, 2019; Leenen *et al.*, 2020).

Despite an increase in cybersecurity awareness training programs, including those aimed at SMEs, and the implementation of security policies, procedures, and technical solutions, cybersecurity incidents still occur at a high frequency in businesses that provide such training (Georgiadou *et al.*, 2020). Although reports indicate that many employees have claimed to understand their company's policies and procedures, knowing alone is not sufficient to eliminate harmful behaviour - SMEs must establish a cybersecurity culture (Huzaizi *et al.*, 2021).

In the context of this study, change management is considered a crucial factor for bringing about the necessary changes required for the successful implementation of DT and BMI, as well as for establishing and sustaining a culture of cybersecurity (Nel & Drevin, 2019). Previous studies have not offered specific guidance on how to effect changes when the cybersecurity culture falls short of the required level for safeguarding information and systems (Uchendu *et al.*, 2021). Hence, cybersecurity culture issues during DT and BMI are at the core matters of this conceptual study, which provides some guidelines for the application of cybersecurity culture in the DT and BMI transformations. Although these guidelines are considered general, the authors' thinking was centered around the applicability of this study to SMEs in South Africa.

DIGITAL TRANSFORMATION AND BUSINESS MODELS INNOVATION

Digital Transformation encompasses a wide range of actions that impact various aspects of an organisation, including IT infrastructure, strategy and business models, value creation with customers and partners, managerial approach, and organisational culture (Pagani 2013; Matt *et al.* 2015; Kane *et al.* 2015; Legner *et al.* 2017). In simpler terms, DT involves redefining job and income creation strategies, adopting a flexible management model to stay competitive, responding quickly to changing demands, reinventing the business to digitise operations and establish extended supply chain relationships, making functional use of the Internet for design, manufacturing, marketing, selling, presenting, and adopting a data-driven management model (Schallmo *et al.*, 2018). DT's impact can be categorised into three dimensions, according to Pousttchi (2017):

• Value creation dimension, which includes the technology's impact on business processes, the overall organisation of a company, and its workforce.

• Value proposition dimension, which includes the impact on the selection of products and services offered to the market and their revenue models.

• The customer interaction dimension, which encompasses all forms and methods of engaging with customers.

A closely related concept of Digital disruption (DD) is described as the provisioning of a new value proposition based on the opportunities that can be addressed with digital technologies (Christensen, 2013). This is a promise for SMEs, among others, to traditionally react faster to market changes and adapt to market needs, either locally or internationally in niche markets (Feichtinger, 2018).

The pertinent literature confirms that DT and DD highly impact an organisation's business activities and success. However, certain factors hinder the DT and DD of SMEs. The costs of digitalisation are considerably higher for SMEs, enhancing the risk of being disrupted by players that use economies of scale and the low marginal costs of platforms. Furthermore, it is estimated that more factors are hindering further investments in the digitalisation of SMEs such as the lack of skills, limited financial options, and lack of know-how.

When the above hindering factors are effectively addressed, DT can be done through Business Model Innovation (BMI) (Garzella *et al.*, 2020) as DT requires companies to rethink and innovate their business models (Bouwman *et al.*, 2019). BMI is a term that has emerged recently and has been defined with various concepts and dimensions. Nevertheless, the fundamental idea of BMI is linked to the competitive advantage and enhanced performance of the organisation (Ranjith, 2016; Evans *et al.*, 2017). While a universally accepted definition of BMI is not yet available, it can be described as an intentional practice that alters the basic components of a company and its business strategy, according to Frankenberger *et al.* (2013).

The literature on BMI has created frameworks and practices to explain the intricate relationship between value creation and value appropriation, as well as to comprehend an organisation's logic for creating value (Massa *et al.*, 2017). In line with these ideas, an increasing number of companies, including SMEs, are now exploring BMI as an alternative or complement to product or process innovation. This is because it can result in a sustainable competitive advantage (Garzella *et al.*, 2020).

Many scholars argue that digital technologies have become powerful forces that compel organisations to adopt new and innovative business models, which has made their capability to innovate increasingly important. Meanwhile, digitalisation provides SMEs with an opportunity to develop the ability to proactively lead BMI, with the help of new technologies. This is because digital technologies can increase the levels of production efficiency, reduce production costs, minimise inventories, and streamline information flows. Therefore, BMIs and DTs are inevitably based on new technologies in today's networked world.

Ernst & Young's (2018) report has highlighted the top challenges for SMEs' DT, which include cybersecurity, higher requirements regarding competencies, and changes in the market environment. While the literature on BMI and cybersecurity is scarce, some authors suggest that the use of ICT can increase opportunities to provide additional value to customers, but the risks associated with cybersecurity may also increase.

Although overall cybersecurity is highly important, organisations repeatedly overlook the human factor upon which cybersecurity security depends. Thus, the misconception that technology alone can solve cybersecurity issues is prevalent, but in reality, cybersecurity is mainly a human issue that remains unaddressed (Metalidou *et al.*, 2014; Nobles, 2022). A study conducted in South Africa on SMEs found that human factors and behaviour are the primary challenges still affecting cybersecurity, leading to a negative impact on cybersecurity culture

(Murphy *et al*., 2022). Therefore, the development of a cybersecurity culture is a significant problem for many South African SMEs seeking to implement effective DT or BMI, as observed in this study.

APPROACH TO THIS STUDY

Exploratory research in social science, such as the one reported here, can be defined in various ways, but at its core, it consists of an attempt to discover something new and interesting by working the way through a research topic (Swedberg, 2020). This exploratory desktop research was aimed at creating a conceptual model related to digital risks facing the Digital Transformation and Business Model Innovation of SMEs and proposing the basic protective measures through developing a cybersecurity culture.

Desktop research is generally associated with literature review and is defined as the process of accessing published secondary data and exclusively relies on published secondary data, which includes books, journals, and articles indexed in many databases, as well as business and research reports. Therefore, secondary data refers to a type of data, which already exists and has been collected in the past for some purpose. All processes of desk research are exercised "in-house" (Jackson, 1994).

In this study, the authors relied on identifying, analysing, synthesising, and critically examining the available data on digital transformation, business model innovation, and cybersecurity culture, primarily in the SME context. The data for this study came from multiple sources such as reviews of literature and published reports and the reviewing was done based on the following objectives:

1. To determine what technologies are used in Digital Transformation and Business Model Innovation.

2. To explore cybersecurity risks of Digital Transformation and Business Model Innovation in the context of SMEs.

3. To suggest general protective measures through the development of a cybersecurity culture in SMEs.

Consequently, the following research questions were answered:

1. What technologies are used in Digital Transformation and Business Model Innovation?

2. What are the cybersecurity risks of Digital Transformation and Business Model Innovation in SMEs?

3. What are general protective measures linked to the development of cybersecurity culture in SMEs?

The major relationships between the key concepts of this study were analysed and the consequential analysis was used to conceptualise cybersecurity culture in SMEs but could also apply to other organisations.

This paper reports on the conceptual part of this study, which will be followed by empirical research that will be reported as soon as it is completed. The paper is further organised as follows: we first discuss technologies used in the context of DT and BMI, followed by the cybersecurity risks related to these technologies, and the suggestion of essential protective measures through the development of a cybersecurity culture conceptual model. The paper ends with concluding remarks and apposite recommendations.

TECHNOLOGIES USED IN DIGITAL TRANSFORMATION THROUGH BUSINESS MODELS INNOVATION

With the advent of digital technology, traditional methods of work are being replaced and companies are now creating highly responsive digital systems that allow for immediate movement of goods from production to consumers upon placing orders. As a result, the era of waiting for sales teams to sell produced goods is a thing of the past (Zaki, 2019), and we are currently in the age of digital business and innovation.

DT and BMI are based on the direct and indirect effects of the application of digital technologies as well as new products and services supported by these technologies. Contemporary technologies offer new potential for comprehensive cognitive and mixed mechanical cognitive tasks in all kinds of organisations. In that regard, the following types of technologies are used (Pousttchi *et al.*, 2019):

• Wide-ranging use of sensors and actuators, including those for audio and video recording.

• Utilisation of mobile communication technologies for networking and automated communication, with extremely low latency (Internet of Things).

• Collection, storage, and analysis of massive data sets using big data techniques.

• Various machine-learning techniques.

• Advanced methods of human-computer interaction.

Stationary devices such as desktop and laptop computers are still DT and BMI basic technologies. However, mobile devices and technologies are increasingly gaining momentum. The communication technologies used in DT and BMI mainly refer to all kinds of mobile communication systems, including 2G/3G/4G/5G mobile networks. It seems that even local area networks (LAN) typically rely on wireless fidelity (Wi-Fi) connections, personal area networks (PAN) and ad-hoc networks on Bluetooth or near-field communication (NFC) (EIST, 2015). Mobile devices used within DT and BMI consist of smartphones, tablets, and wearables.

The rapid increase in the amount of available data allows companies of all sizes to analyse insights and make informed decisions in real-time. Data technologies, including established database technologies, distributed file systems, blockchain, big data, and analytics, are commonly used in DT and BMI across organizations. Companies transitioning to digital utilise a combination of multiple technologies, business process automation, and machine-to-machine interactions through IoT to develop intelligent systems (Bolton *et al.*, 2018).

The human-computer interface (HCI) technologies used in DT and BMI include multi-touch displays, virtual and augmented reality (VR and AR) conversational user interfaces, virtual assistants, and gesture control. 3D printing is extensively used by, for example, building companies to build complex three-dimensional structures and integrate functions.

The application of Artificial Intelligence (AI) is a potent instrument in DT and BMI that has already begun to influence all industries. McKinsey (2018) predicts that by 2030, approximately 70% of companies will have integrated some form of AI, particularly machine learning, and even more specifically, deep learning. As per available reports, SMEs use AI mainly close to production in conjunction with Cloud computing (Hansen & Bogh, 2021), which requires cybersecurity attention.

Cloud Computing (CC) belongs to technologies that are extensively used for boosting economic activities, particularly by SMEs, as CC services are extensively used for collaboration. For example, just-in-time/just-in-sequence production planning, based on real-time consumption, can be achieved by an integrated Cloud-based enterprise resources planning (ERP) system for the end-to-end supply chain. This enables suppliers to plan their disposition and production based on real-time data (Junge, 2019).

Social Media is being utilised by executives and employees across all industries to improve customer relationships, internal processes, and value propositions (Westerman *et al.*, 2014; Agnihotri, 2021). For instance, the primary goal of Social Media marketing is to generate content that can attract more consumers

(Onețiu, 2020). Almost half of the South African population, which is approximately 25 million users in 2020, are active on social media, with over 30 million individuals using it (Design-IT, 2022). Many of these users are SME owners or employees.

These novel technologies go beyond automating basic processes, fulfilling information requirements, or influencing business strategy, which was the traditional role of IT in past periods (Ward *et al*., 1990). They have the potential to reshape the entire business strategy by ensuring the effectiveness, flexibility, dependability, and predictability of fundamental operations, while also enabling the quick development and deployment of fast innovations in response to or anticipation of customers' demands (Zaki, 2019). Electronic commerce has emerged as a vital innovation in the past two decades and has become an indispensable technology in the business world. To thrive in the current competitive economic environment, SMEs, like other businesses, have had to embrace e-commerce (Rahayu & Day, 2015).

All these technologies should be protected by appropriate cybersecurity technologies such as hardware and software firewalls, endpoint protection software, application security software, Intrusion Detection System (IDS) and Intrusion Prevention System (IPS), and Data Loss Prevention (DLP) & Data encryption technologies. However, cybersecurity risks tend to go far above the use of these technologies, which is the topic of the following sections.

CYBERSECURITY RISKS OF DIGITAL TRANSFORMATION AND BUSINESS MODEL INNOVATION

Cybersecurity is now mission-critical to the way businesses of all sizes operate around the world. Hence, it is nowadays imperative to understand that cybersecurity enables organisations to function, meaning that cybersecurity plays a role in the way business is done (Nasdaq, 2021).

Small and medium-sized enterprises face distinct risks, and their limited financial and non-financial resources make them more vulnerable, like larger organisations (Fielder *et al*., 2016). However, underestimating cybersecurity risks can have severe consequences, affecting both tangible and intangible assets and potentially leading to a business failure (Hollman & Mohammad-Zadeh, 1984). Therefore, it is crucial to comprehend the cybersecurity threats that SMEs face, as this understanding can aid them in attaining beneficial digital transformation and business model innovation (Alahmari & Duncan, 2021).

Recently, cybersecurity has become a global challenge for many companies of all sizes wanting to transform digital business activities and models. In the first 2 months of 2022 alone, there were reported 2,12,485 cyberattacks, more than the entirety of 2018. The figures rose more sharply through the COVID pandemic, with reported cybercrime increasing from 3,94,499 cases in 2019 to 11,58,208 in 2020 and 14,02,809 in 2021 (AAG, 2022). South Africa has now registered the largest year-on-year increase in cybercrime and has seen an increase of more than 200% in cyber-attacks since 2019.

Cyberattacks have various motivations globally, including financial gain, political reasons, accessing private information, identity theft, cryptocurrency theft, destruction to infrastructure, and others such as manufacturing, banking, and hospitals which provide critical services to society and are often the victims of such attacks (Sandhu, 2021). This highlights the high cybersecurity risks faced by SMEs looking to advance digitally or already undergoing digital transformation (DT) or business model innovation (BMI). These risks include loss of confidentiality, integrity, or availability of information and data, which can negatively impact organisational operations, assets, individuals, other organisations, and even the nation (NISTIR 8286, 2020; ISO Guide 73, 2009).

In general, cyber risks refer to the possibility of financial loss, operational disruption, or damage due to the failure of certain digital technologies or systems used for operational or informational purposes within an organisation. This risk arises when network systems are compromised through unauthorised access, use, disruption, or modification of organisational information systems. Therefore, the main risks that hinder the wider adoption of DT and BMI technologies by SMEs include data security concerns, interoperability issues with existing IT systems, and a lack of control (Schwertner, 2017).

Although ICT is beneficial for SMEs, it also has its drawbacks that cybercriminals can exploit. For instance, Cloud computing is a common technology used by SMEs, but it can become a prime target for cybercriminals if the providers' vulnerabilities have been exposed. According to recent reports, SMEs are the primary target for cyberattacks, mainly due to their weaker defence techniques compared to large firms. This is due to factors such as less expertise, unknown outsourcing, and outdated security methods (Barlette *et al.*, 2017; Kaufman, 2009).

However, a significant challenge for SMEs is the misconception that their small size makes them immune to cyber threats (Barlette *et al.*, 2017). Furthermore, studies indicate that SME managers and employees often lack knowledge and awareness regarding the importance of security tools, policies, and procedures, leading to lower adoption of cybersecurity measures (Watad *et al.*, 2018). Additionally, some SMEs may recognize the potential for cyberattacks but lack the necessary skills, resources, and determination to effectively protect themselves, making them vulnerable to such threats (Renaud & Weir, 2016).

Considering these factors, the behaviour and commitment of individuals within SMEs play a crucial role in safeguarding organisational information assets. Training, education, and awareness programs are therefore essential for enhancing cybersecurity practices (Kaur & Mustafa, 2013; Gundu, 2019). These efforts contribute to building a cybersecurity culture, and the absence of such a culture within SMEs is a significant cybersecurity risk (Kabanda *et al.*, 2018).

The connection between users' conduct and their attitude towards cybersecurity awareness is substantial (Alahmari & Duncan, 2021). This is a crucial component of cybersecurity culture (Advenica, 2020). Therefore, cultivating an effective cybersecurity culture in businesses, including SMEs, is a comprehensive solution that does not depend on the size of the company or the specific technologies employed - it greatly influences the secure utilisation of these technologies (Wamala, 2011; Gcaza *et al.*, 2015; Reegård *et al*, 2019).

A BASIC PREVENTATIVE MEASURE: DEVELOPING CYBERSECURITY CULTURE

Previous research on cybersecurity culture has not provided specific recommendations on how to implement changes needed to protect organisational systems and information. SMEs have often been overlooked in cybersecurity culture frameworks, and it is essential to develop approaches that cater to their specific needs. One framework is unlikely to work for all types of organisations, so it is necessary to consider the multiple perspectives of SMEs within the cybersecurity culture research (Uchendu *et al.*, 2021). This study aims to address this gap in the literature by focusing on the role of humans, who are responsible for developing a cybersecurity culture in SMEs.

Implementing effective cybersecurity measures is particularly important but is nowadays challenging since there are more digital devices than people. At the same time, attackers are becoming more innovative in their criminal endeavours. In this environment, technology alone cannot be a cushion against cyber threats, instead, humans should occupy a central stage through the development of a cybersecurity culture (Gcaza, *et al*, 2015).

Cybersecurity culture (CSC) is defined as the beliefs, assumptions, attitudes, values, perceptions, and knowledge that people have about cybersecurity and how these manifest in their interaction with ICT. A strong cyber security culture changes the mindsets of people and their security behaviour (ENISA, 2018). Therefore, the attitudes, assumptions, beliefs, values, and knowledge of people must promote efficiency, innovation, and economic prosperity while encouraging safety, security, business confidentiality, privacy, quality, and civil liberties when using cyberspace (NIST, 2014). In short, developing an appropriate cybersecurity culture could address many of the behavioural issues that underpin cybersecurity breaches in SMEs. By having developed a cybersecurity culture where employees intuitively protect the company's informational assets, SMEs could improve their overall cybersecurity posture (Dojkovski *et al.*, 2007; Santos-Olmo *et al.*, 2016; ENISA, 2019).

Cybersecurity culture by its nature needs to be cultivated rather than rigidly designed (Uchendu *et al.*, 2021) and this study subscribes to this suggestion. Cybersecurity culture has many facets such as dimensions, layers, factors, practices, implementation strategies, education, training and awareness, and forms of delivery. Elaboration of all these facets will require much more space than available here, hence this section will describe one of the crucial aspects of cybersecurity culture that is relevant to SMEs: practices for building cybersecurity (Fig. **1**). According to the pertinent literature, these practises consist of several steps: (1) Securing management support; (2) Having sound cybersecurity policies; (3) Organising continual cybersecurity awareness and training sessions; (4) Achieving involvement of the entire workforce and organise effective communication; and (5) Learning from experience (Reegård *et al*, 2019).

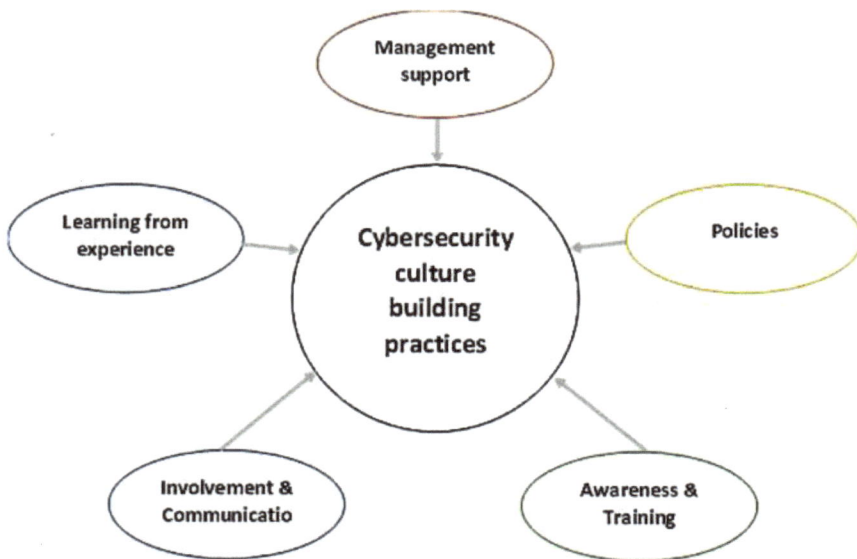

Fig. (1). A model for cybersecurity culture-building practices (Source: Authors, based on Reegård *et al.*, 2019).

The support of management can take different forms, such as providing financial resources, promoting cybersecurity initiatives, or taking an active role in organising the cybersecurity function and monitoring its progress. Hence, management support is crucial in establishing and sustaining a culture of cybersecurity in an organisation. For example, top management's visible support and active involvement are critical to the development and enforcement of cybersecurity policies (Karyada *et al.*, 2005).

Creating an internal policy is an important practice for building a cybersecurity culture, as it demonstrates management's commitment to cybersecurity and emphasises its importance. Such policies can improve employees' ability to manage cybersecurity issues when they are aware of the organisation's cybersecurity policies (Li *et al.*, 2019). These policies also serve as general guidelines for establishing a suitable culture (Knapp *et al.*, 2009). It is crucial to strike a balance between management's and employees' perspectives when crafting cybersecurity policies to ensure they are practical and effective.

Training and awareness sessions for the workforce are crucial in shaping cybersecurity culture and mitigating threats caused by human vulnerabilities. Hence, these sessions serve as a cornerstone for building a cybersecurity culture (Metalidou *et al.*, 2014). This is supported by an ENISA (2010) report which suggests that cybersecurity awareness programmes should aim to bring about positive changes in attitude and behaviour, gain and maintain the trust and satisfaction of the audience and management, and ultimately minimise the number and impact of cybersecurity breaches.

To enhance cybersecurity awareness, an organisation needs to provide training that is specifically designed for the target audience as people tend to understand and process information about risks based on their cognitive and cultural biases (Thsohou *et al*, 2015). Therefore, according to Van Niekerk & Von Solms (2010), it cannot be assumed that the average employee has sufficient knowledge to perform their job securely. This highlights the importance of cybersecurity awareness training.

According to Lin and Wittmer's (2017) research, employee participation can enhance cybersecurity if they are motivated to participate, which fosters a proactive approach. Encouraging horizontal participation, i.e., peer-to-peer involvement, is considered one of the most effective ways to boost motivation (Ruighaver *et al.*, 2007), while two-way vertical communication between management and employees is essential to overcoming the 'us vs. them' commonly observed mentality (Ashenden & Sasse, 2013).

An essential aspect of building a strong cybersecurity culture is to learn from experience. To achieve this, organisations can use maturity models to assess their current level of cybersecurity culture and identify areas that require improvement. Additionally, incident reporting systems serve as a crucial mechanism for sharing information on incidents and preventing their reoccurrence or mitigating their damage (Reegård et al., 2019).

Finally, verifying specific outcomes is employed to confirm or disprove existing assumptions about an organisation's security (Kearney & Kruger, 2016). Auditing is an instance of this mechanism that can enhance an organisation's awareness of its internal cybersecurity environment (Reegård et al., 2019). On the other hand, organisations may become trapped in an external focus when undergoing an external audit, where their primary goal is to pass the audit instead of attaining the cybersecurity culture they require (Ruighaver et al., 2007).

The above are some of the crucial elements for building a cybersecurity culture. A more comprehensive guide to developing an effective cybersecurity culture in organisations of all types, including SMEs, must be based on a comprehensive analysis of the role of human factors in cybersecurity, followed by an analysis of different training methods used in cybersecurity awareness programmes, which is out of scope of this study.

CONCLUSION

This exploratory, conceptual desktop research was the first phase of a two-fold study aimed at creating a conceptual model that includes cybersecurity risks facing SMEs, wishing to perform or are in the process of DT and BMI, and basic protective measures through developing an effective cybersecurity culture. This is done by meeting the objectives set in this study by reviewing the contemporary literature.

Following the first objective, we have described the types of technologies used within the notion of DT and BMI. Then the second objective was fulfilled by exploring and reporting the cybersecurity risks related to DT and BMI. Finally, the third objective was met by suggesting preventative measures, i.e., we have described how to start building a cybersecurity culture in SMEs by presenting a Model for cybersecurity culture practices.

The main contribution of this study is seen through exploring and describing cybersecurity issues of DT and BMI and recommending to SMEs the basic protective measures through building an effective cybersecurity culture. Cybersecurity should not be an afterthought as new business initiatives take place - it should be prioritised at the beginning or in the implementation strategies of

DT and BMI. In a nutshell, this study concludes that embedding cybersecurity, through the development of cybersecurity culture into innovation is essential. While the DT-related cybersecurity issues are explored and reported to some extent, cybersecurity issues related to BMI are rarely explored and the reports are almost non-existent. This gives pioneering attributes to this study.

The current phase of our study is limited to a purely theoretical approach without empirical data, which we suggest should be addressed in the next phase of research. We agree with the recommendation of Uchendu *et al.* (2021) that untested conceptual models should be subjected to future studies to test their external validity in various organisations. However, despite this limitation, we strongly advise SMEs to prioritise the development of an effective cybersecurity culture to enhance their overall cybersecurity posture.

GLOSSARY

Cybersecurity	Cybersecurity refers to the practice of safeguarding computer systems, networks, devices, and digital data from unauthorised access, attacks, damage, or theft. It aims to ensure the confidentiality, integrity, and availability of digital resources while minimising the risks associated with potential cyber incidents.
Cybersecurity awareness	Cybersecurity awareness refers to the level of understanding and consciousness individuals, employees, and organisations possess regarding potential cyber threats and best practices for mitigating them. It involves educating individuals about various cyber risks, tactics used by cybercriminals, and methods to protect digital assets and sensitive information.
Cybersecurity culture	Cybersecurity culture refers to the collective mindset, values, attitudes, and behaviours of individuals within an organisation regarding cybersecurity practices. It involves fostering a proactive and security-conscious environment where all employees understand the importance of cybersecurity, actively participate in risk management, and consistently follow best practices to protect digital assets and sensitive data.
Cybersecurity initiatives	Cybersecurity initiatives refer to planned and organised efforts undertaken by organisations to enhance their cybersecurity posture and protect digital assets from cyber threats. These initiatives encompass a wide range of activities, strategies, and projects aimed at identifying vulnerabilities, implementing security measures, and promoting a culture of cybersecurity awareness.
Cybersecurity risk	Cybersecurity risk refers to the potential for adverse events or incidents stemming from cyber threats that could result in the compromise, damage, unauthorised access, or loss of digital assets, data, or information. It encompasses the likelihood of cyberattacks, data breaches, malware infections, and other malicious activities that could impact an organization's confidentiality, integrity, or availability of resources

Cybersecurity threat	A cybersecurity threat refers to any potential danger or malicious activity that has the capability to exploit vulnerabilities in computer systems, networks, or digital assets. It encompasses a wide range of intentional or unintentional actions, tactics, techniques, or tools used by cybercriminals or malicious actors to compromise data confidentiality, integrity, or availability.
Cloud Computing	Cloud computing refers to the delivery of computing resources, including servers, storage, databases, networking, software, and analytics, over the internet ("the cloud"). This model allows users to access and utilise these resources on-demand, eliminating the need for owning and maintaining physical infrastructure.
Digital Transformation (DT)	DT is the process of leveraging technology to fundamentally change and improve the way organizations operate, deliver value, and interact with their stakeholders. It involves adopting digital technologies, strategies, and business models to enhance efficiency, innovation, and customer experiences.
Information and communication technologies (ICT)	ICT refer to a broad range of technologies used for gathering, storing, processing, transmitting, and managing information. ICT encompasses hardware, software, networks, and digital technologies that enable communication, data sharing, and information exchange. It includes tools such as computers, smartphones, internet services, telecommunications networks, software applications, and digital media platforms.
Social Media	Social media refers to online platforms and websites that enable users to create, share, and interact with content, information, and media in a collaborative and interactive manner. These platforms facilitate the exchange of text, images, videos, and other multimedia content among individuals, groups, or organisations.

REFERENCES

AAG (2022) The Latest 2022 Cyber Crime Statistics (updated November 2022). Available from: https: //aag-it. com/the -latest -2022 -cyber- crime -statistics/

Advenica (2020) Security culture - an important part of cybersecurity. Available from: https: //advenica .com/en/ blog/2020 -01-23 /security -culture -an-important -part- of-cyberse curity

Agnihotri, R (2021) From sales force automation to digital transformation: how social media, social CRM, and artificial intelligence technologies are influencing the sales,. *in Research Agenda for Sales Monograph Book.*

Alahmari, A & Duncan, B (2021) Cybersecurity risk management in small and medium-sized enterprises: A systematic review of recent evidence. *13th International Conference on Electronics, Computers and Artificial Intelligence (ECAI).*

Appio, FP, Frattini, F, Messeni Petruzzelli, A & Neirotti, P (2020) Digital transformation and innovation management: A synthesis of existing research and an agenda for future studies. *J Prod Innov Manage*

Ashenden, D & Sasse, A (2013) CISOs and organisational culture: Their own worst enemy? *Comput Secur,* 39, 396-405.
[http://dx.doi.org/10.1016/j.cose.2013.09.004]

Barlette, Y, Gundolf, K & Jaouen, A (2017) CEOs' information security behavior in SMEs: Does ownership matter? Syst. d'. *Inf Manage,* 22, 7-45.

Bolton, RN, McColl-Kennedy, JR, Cheung, L, Gallan, A, Orsingher, C, Witell, L & Zaki, M (2018) Customer experience challenges: Bringing together digital, physical and social realms. *J Serv Manag,* 29, 776-808.
[http://dx.doi.org/10.1108/JOSM-04-2018-0113]

Bughin, J & van Zeebroeck, N (2017) The best response to digital disruption. *MIT Sloan Manag Rev,* 58, 80-6.

Bouwman, H, Nikou, S & de Reuver, M (2019) Digitalization, business models, and SMEs: How do business model innovation practices improve performance of digitalizing SMEs? *Telecomm Policy,* 43, 101828. [http://dx.doi.org/10.1016/j.telpol.2019.101828]

Brehmer, M, Podoynitsyna, K & Langerak, F (2018) Sustainable business models as boundary-spanning systems of value transfers. *J Clean Prod* 172, 4514-31.

Caputo, A., Fiorentino, R. & Garzella, S. (2018) From the boundaries of management to the management of boundaries: business processes, capabilities and negotiations. *Bus Process Manag J*, 25(3), 391-413. [http://dx.doi.org/10.1108/BPMJ-11-2017-0334]

Christensen, CM (2013) *The innovator's dilemma: When new technologies cause great firms to fail.*Harvard Business Review Press, Boston, Mass.

Cozzolino, A, Verona, G & Rothaermel, FT (2018) Unpacking the disruption process: New technology, business models, and incumbent adaptation. *J Manage Stud,* 55, 1166-202. [http://dx.doi.org/10.1111/joms.12352]

De Maggio, MC, Mastrapasqua, M, Tesei, M, Chittaro, A & Setola, R (2019) How to improve the security awareness in complex organizations. *European Journal for Security Research,* 4, 33-49. [http://dx.doi.org/10.1007/s41125-017-0028-2]

Ayyagari, M, Beck, T & Demirguc-Kunt, A (2007) A small and medium enterprises across the globe. *Small Bus Econ,* 29, 415-34. [http://dx.doi.org/10.1007/s11187-006-9002-5]

Design-IT (2022) Social media stats in South Africa in 2022, Available from: https://dezignit.co.za/social-media-stats-in-south-africa/#:~:text=How%20many%20people%20in%20South,25%25million%20users

Dojkovski, S, Lichtenstein, S & Warren, MJ (2007) Fostering information security culture in small and medium size enterprises: An interpretive study in australia. *In: ECIS,* 1560-71.

EIST (2015) Routing Protocols for IEEE 802.11-Based Mesh Networks, Encyclopedia of Information Science and Technology, Third Edition.

ENISA (2010) The new users' guide: How to raise information security awareness. Available from: https://www.enisa.europa.eu/publications/archive/copy_of_new-users-guide/at_download/fullReport

ENISA (2018) Available from: https://www.enisa.europa.eu/publications/cyber-security-culture-in-organisations/at_download/fullReport#:~:text=Cybersecurity%20Culture%20(CSC)%20of%20organizations,behaviour%20with%20information%20technologies

ENISA (2019) Available from: https://www.enisa.europa.eu/publications/cybersecurity-cultureguideline--behavioural-aspects-of-cybersecurity/

Ernst & Young *Digital change in Austrian medium-sized companies.* Available from: http://www.ey.com/Publication/vwLUAssets/EYStudie_%E2%80%9EDigitaler_Wandel_im_Mittelstand%E2%80%9C_-_M%C3%A4rz_2018/$FILE/EY%20Digitalisierungsstudie%20Oesterreich%202018.pdf

Evans, S, Vladimirova, D, Holgado, M, Van Fossen, K, Yang, M, Silva, EA & Barlow, CY (2017) Business model innovation for sustainability: Towards a unified perspective for creation of sustainable business models. *Bus Strategy Environ,* 26, 597-608. [http://dx.doi.org/10.1002/bse.1939]

Feichtinger, G (2018) Digitalization in SME: A framework to get from strategy to action, a master's thesis submitted for the degree of "Master of Business Administration". *WU Executive Academy.* Vienna, July 16, 2018.

Fielder, A, Panaousis, E, Malacaria, P, Hankin, C & Smeraldi, F (2016) Decision support approaches for cyber security investment. *Decis Support Syst,* 86, 13-23.

[http://dx.doi.org/10.1016/j.dss.2016.02.012]

Fjeldstad, ØD & Snow, CC (2018) Business models and organization design. *Long Range Plann,* 51, 32-9. [http://dx.doi.org/10.1016/j.lrp.2017.07.008]

Foss, NJ & Saebi, T Fifteen years of research on business model innovation: how far have we come, and where should we go? *J Manag,* 43, 200-227.

Frankenberger, K, T Weiblen, M Csik and O Gassmann (2013) The 4I-framework of business model innovation: A structured view on process phases and challenges. *Int J Prod Dev,* 18(3/4), 249–73.

Garzella, S, Fiorentino, R, Caputo, A & Lardo, A (2020) Business model innovation in SMEs: the role of boundaries in the digital era, Technology Analysis & Strategic Management. 33, 31-43.

Gcaza, N, Solms, R & Vuuren, J (2015) An ontology for a national cybersecurity culture environment. *Proceedings of the 9th International Symposium on Human Aspects of Information Security & Assurance,* 1-10.

Georgiadou, A, Mouzakitis, S, Bounas, K & Askounis, D (2020) A cyber security culture framework for assessing organization readiness. *J Comput Inf Syst,* 1, 12.

Ghernaouti, S & Wanner, B (2018) Research and education as key success factors for developing a cybersecurity culture. *Best Pract,* 539-52. [http://dx.doi.org/10.1007/978-3-658-21655-9_38]

Gundu, T (2019) Acknowledging and reducing the knowing and doing gap in employee cybersecurity compliance *in ICCWS 2019 14th Int Conf Cyber Warf Secur,,* 94-102.

Hansen, EB & Bogh, S (2020) Artificial intelligence and internet of things in small and medium-sized enterprises: A survey *Journal of Manufacturing Systems,* 58, 362-72.

Hollman, KW & Mohammad-Zadeh, S (1984) Risk management in small business. *J Small Bus Manag,* 22, 7-55.

Huzaizi, AHA, Siti, NAAT, Bahari, TA, Manan, KA & Mubin, NNA (2021) Cyber-security culture towards digital marketing communications among small and medium-sized (SME) entrepreneurs. *Asian Culture and History,* 13, 20.

IFC (2021) IFC stats as found in "SME's make up the bulk of labour with estimates of 60% of the work force. https://www.news24.com/fin24/partnercontent/the-essential-role-of-smes-in-the-economy-20220510

Ismail, WBW & Yusof, M (2018) Mitigation strategies for unintentional insider threats on information leaks. *International Journal of Security and Its Applications,* 12, 37-46. [http://dx.doi.org/10.14257/ijsia.2018.12.1.03]

ISO Guide 73 (2009) ISO Guide 73:2009 risk management — vocabulary. Available at https://www.iso.org/standard/44651.html

Jackson, P (1994) *Desk Research.* Kogan.

Jeza, S & Mpele Lekhanya, L (2022) The influence of digital transformation on the growth of small and medium enterprises in South Africa. *Probl Perspect Manag,* 20, 297-309. [http://dx.doi.org/10.21511/ppm.20(3).2022.24]

Junge, AL (2019) Digital transformation technologies as an enabler for sustainable logistics and supply chain processes – an exploratory framework. *Braz J Oper Prod Manag,* 16, 462-72.

Kabanda, S, Tanner, M & Kent, C (2018) Exploring SME cybersecurity practices in developing countries. *J Organ Comput Electron Commerce,* 28, 269-82. [http://dx.doi.org/10.1080/10919392.2018.1484598]

Kane, GC, Palmer, D, Phillips, AN, Kiron, D & Buckley, N (2015) Strategy, not technology, drives digital transformation, mit sloan management review *MIT Sloan Management Review.* Available from: https://sloanreview.mit.edu/projects

Kearney, WD & Kruger, HA (2016) Can perceptual differences account for enigmatic information security behaviour in an organisation? *Comput Secur,* 61, 46-58.
[http://dx.doi.org/10.1016/j.cose.2016.05.006]

Karyda, M, Kiountouzis, E & Kokolakis, S (2005) Information systems security policies: A contextual perspective. *Comput Secur,* 24, 246-60.
[http://dx.doi.org/10.1016/j.cose.2004.08.011]

Leenen, L, van Vuren, JJ & van Vuren, A-MJ (2020) Cybersecurity and cybercrime combatting culture for african police services, cybersecurity and cybercrime combatting culture for african police services.*Human-Centric Computing in a Data-Driven Society HCC 2020 IFIP Advances in Information and Communication Technology* Springer.

Lin, C & Wittmer, JLS (2017) Proactive information security behavior and individual creativity: Effects of group culture and descentralized IT governance *2017 IEEE International Conference on Intelligence and Security Informatics.*
[http://dx.doi.org/10.1109/ISI.2017.8004865]

Lindgren, P (2017) Advanced business model innovation. *Wirel Pers Commun,* 95, 127-44.
[http://dx.doi.org/10.1007/s11277-017-4420-z]

Kaufman, LM (2009) Data security in the world of cloud computing. *IEEE Secur Priv,* 7, 61-4.
[http://dx.doi.org/10.1109/MSP.2009.87]

Kaur, J & Mustafa, N (2013) Examining the effects of knowledge, attitude and behaviour on information security awareness: A case on SME," in 2013 Int. Conf. Res. *Innov Inf Syst IEEE,,* 286-90.

Li, L, He, W, Xu, L, Ash, I, Anwar, M & Yuan, X (2019) Investigating the impact of cybersecurity policy awareness on employees' cybersecurity behavior. *Int J Inf Manage,* 45, 13-24.
[http://dx.doi.org/10.1016/j.ijinfomgt.2018.10.017]

Legner, C, Eymann, T, Hess, T, Matt, C, Böhmann, T, Drews, P, Mädche, A, Urbach, N & Ahlemann, F (2017) Digitalization: Opportunity and challenge for the business and information systems engineering community. *Business and Information Systems Engineering,* 59, 301-8.

Massa, L, Tucci, CL & Afuah, A (2017) A critical assessment of business model research. *Acad Management Ann,* 11, 73-104.
[http://dx.doi.org/10.5465/annals.2014.0072]

Masroor, N & Asim, M (2019) SMEs in the contemporary era of global competition. *Procedia Comput Sci,* 158, 632-41.
[http://dx.doi.org/10.1016/j.procs.2019.09.097]

Matt, C, Hess, T & Benlian, A (2015) Digital transformation strategies, business and information systems engineering. 339-43.

McKinsey Global Institute (2018) *Notes from the AI frontier: modeling the impact of AI on the world economy.* Available from: www.mckinsey.com/featured-insights/artificial-intelligence/notes-from-the- ai-frontier-modeling-the-impact-of-ai-on-the-world-economy

Metalidou, E, Marinagi, C, Trivellas, P, Eberhagen, N, Skourlas, C & Giannakopoulos, G (2014) The human factor of information security: Unintentional damage perspective. *Procedia Soc Behav Sci,* 147, 424-8.
[http://dx.doi.org/10.1016/j.sbspro.2014.07.133]

Mielcarek, M & Dymitrowski, A (2022) Business model innovation based on new technologies – is it resources driven and dependent? European Business Review, Article publication date: 1 June 2022 Reprints & Permissions, Issue publication date: 9 August 2022.

Murphy, C, Mtegha, CQ, Chigona, W & Tuyeni, TT (2022) Factors affecting compliance with the national cybersecurity. *African Conference on Information Systems and Technology.*

Nasdaq (2021) Cybersecurity & Innovation: The Key to a Secure Future. Available from: https://indexes.nasdaqomx.com/docs/Cybersecurity%20Innovation.pdf

National Small Business Act (1996) Available from: https://www.gov.za/documents/national-small-busine-s-act#:~:text=The%20National%20Small%20Business%20Act,provide%20for%20matters%20incidental%20thereto

Nel, F & Drevin, L (2019) Key elements of an information security culture in organisations Information &. *Comput Secur,* 27, 146-64.

NIST (2014) *Framework for improving Critical Infrastructure Cybersecurity, Version 10, 2014.* National Institute of Standards and Technology.

NISTIR 8286 (2014) Integrating cybersecurity and enterprise risk management (ERM), National Institute of Standards and Technology.

Njoroge, GM (2020) Human factor affecting favourable cybersecurity culture: A case of small and medium-sized enterprises (SMEs), *Masteres Thesis*The University of Nairobi, School of Computing and Informatics.

Nugroho, MA, Susilo, AZ, Fajar, MA & Rahmawati, D (2017) Exploratory study of SMEs technology adoption readiness factors. *Procedia Comput Sci,* 124, 329-36. [http://dx.doi.org/10.1016/j.procs.2017.12.162]

OECD (2014) *Financing SMEs and entrepreneurs 2014: An OECD scoreboard, Organisation for Economic Co-operation and Development.* OECD Publishing, Paris.

Onețiu, DD (2020) The impact of Social Media adoption by companies. *Digital transformation, Studia Universitatis —Vasile Goldisۡ Arad Economics Series,* 30, 2.

Pagani, M (2013) Digital business strategy and value creation: Framing the dynamic cycle of control points. *MIS Quarterly,* 617-32.

Pousttchi, K (2017) Digitale Transformation, In: Gronau, N., Becker, J., Kliewer, N., Leimeister, J.M., Overhage, S. (eds.), Encyclopaedia of Business Informatics.

Pousttchi, K, Gleiss, A, Buzzi, B & Kohlhagen, M (2019) Technology impact types for digital transformation. *2019 IEEE 21st Conference on Business Informatics (CBI).*

Prasanna, RPIR, Jayasundara, JMSB, Naradda Gamage, SK, Ekanayake, EMS, Rajapakshe, PSK & Abeyrathne, GAKNJ (2019) Sustainability of SMEs in the competition: A systemic review on technological challenges and SME Performance. *J Open Innov,* 5, 100. [http://dx.doi.org/10.3390/joitmc5040100]

Pucihar, A, Lenart, G, Kljajić Borštnar, M, Vidmar, D & Marolt, M (2019) Drivers and outcomes of business model innovation—micro, small and medium-sized enterprises perspective. *Sustainability,* 11, 344. [http://dx.doi.org/10.3390/su11020344]

Rahayu, R & Day, J (2015) Determinant factors of e-commerce adoption by SMEs in developing country: Evidence from Indonesia, Procedia-Social. *Behav Sci (Basel),* 195, 142-50.

Ranjith, VK (2016) Business models and competitive advantage. *Procedia Econ Finance,* 37, 203-7. [http://dx.doi.org/10.1016/S2212-5671(16)30114-9]

Reegård, K, Blackett, C & Katta, V (2019) The Concept of Cybersecurity Culture. *29ᵗʰ European Safety and Reliability Conference (ESREL).* Hannover, Germany. [http://dx.doi.org/10.3850/978-981-11-2724-3_0761-cd]

Reim, W, Astrom, J & Eriksson, O (2020) Implementation of artificial intelligence (AI): A roadmap for business model innovation, implementation of artificial intelligence (AI): A Roadmap for Business Model Innovation. 180-91.

Renaud, K & Weir, GRS (2016) Cybersecurity and the unbearability of uncertainty, in 2016 cybersecurity cyberforensics conf. *IEEE,* 137-43.

Ruighaver, AB, Maynard, SB & Chang, S (2007) Organisational security culture: Extending the end-user perspective. *Comput Secur,* 26, 56-62.

[http://dx.doi.org/10.1016/j.cose.2006.10.008]

Santos-Olmo, A, Sánchez, L, Caballero, I, Camacho, S & Fernandez-Medina, E (2016) The importance of the security culture in SMEs as regards the correct management of the security of their assets. *Future Internet,* 8, 30.
[http://dx.doi.org/10.3390/fi8030030]

Schallmo, D, Willams, CA & Boardman, L (2018) Digital transformation of business models-best practice, enabler, and roadmap. *International Journal of Innovation Management,* 21, 1740014.

Sandhu, K (2021) Advancing Cybersecurity for Digital Transformation: Opportunities and Challenges.*Handbook of Research on Advancing Cybersecurity for Digital Transformation.* IGI Global.
[http://dx.doi.org/10.4018/978-1-7998-6975-7.ch001]

Schwertner, K (2017) Digital transformation of business. *Trakia J Sci,* 15 (Suppl. 1), 388-93.
[http://dx.doi.org/10.15547/tjs.2017.s.01.065]

Skog, DA, Wimelius, H & Sandberg, J (2018) Digital disruption. *Bus Inf Syst Eng,* 60, 431-7.
[http://dx.doi.org/10.1007/s12599-018-0550-4]

Swedberg, R (2020) Exploratory Research. *The Production of Knowledge: Enhancing Progress in Social Science.*Cambridge University Press.
[http://dx.doi.org/10.1017/9781108762519.002]

Tsohou, A, Karyda, M & Kokolakis, S (2015) Analyzing the role of cognitive and cultural biases in the internalization of information security policies: Recommendations for information security awareness programs. *Comput Secur,* 52, 128-41.
[http://dx.doi.org/10.1016/j.cose.2015.04.006]

Uchendu, B, Nurse, JRC, Bada, M & Furnell, S (2021) Developing a cyber security culture: Current practices and future needs. *Comput Secur,* 109, 102387.
[http://dx.doi.org/10.1016/j.cose.2021.102387]

Van Niekerk, JF & Von Solms, R (2010) *Information security culture: A management perspective, Computer Security,* 29, 476-86.

Wamala, F (2011) *ITU National Cybersecurity Strategy Guide.* Available from:
http://onlinelibrary.wiley.com/doi/10.1002/cbdv.200490137/

Ward, J, Griffiths, P & Whitmore, P (1990) *Strategic Planning for Information Systems.* Wiley, Chichester.

Watad, M, Washah, S & Perez, C (2018) IT Security Threats and Challenges for Small Firms: Managers' Perceptions. *Int J Acad Bus World,* 12, 2018.

Westerman, G, Bonnet, D & Mcafee, A (2014) The nine elements of digital transformation. *MIT Sloan Manag Rev,* 55, 1-6.

Zaki, M (2019) Digital transformation: Harnessing digital technologies for the next generation of services. *J Serv Mark,* 33, 429-35.
[http://dx.doi.org/10.1108/JSM-01-2019-0034]

Ziółkowska, MJ (2021) *Digital Transformation and Marketing Activities in Small and Medium-Sized Enterprises Sustain* 2512.
[http://dx.doi.org/10.3390/su13052512]

CHAPTER 3

Assessing SMEs' Business Model Innovation Readiness

Cecil Kgoetiane[1,*]

[1] *Department of Informatics, Faculty of ICT, Tshwane University of Technology, Pretoria, South Africa*

Abstract: This chapter assesses business model innovation readiness for South African SMEs. The assessment is based on the perspective of two challenges that SMEs went through pre-, during, and post-novel coronavirus disease of 2019 (COVID-19). The challenges are about the readiness to innovate the SMEs' business models and grip disruptive technologies such as Intelligent Analytics (IA). To investigate the challenges identified, the chapter expands on IA. In considering IA, four major areas of IA are synthesized. Importantly, IA is about smarter ways of doing business across different sectors. Society 5.0 and the fourth industrial revolution plus (4IR+) complement IA, as the chapter proposes. By and large, the novel COVID-19 accelerated the adoption of disruptive technologies. The chapter concludes by considering the role of the SMEs' owner-managers in embracing the technology.

Keywords: Business Model Innovation, Disruptive Technology, Growth, Industry 4.0, Intelligent Analytics, SMEs.

INTRODUCTION

The chapter looks into two challenges facing Small and Medium Enterprises (SMEs) pre-, during, and post-novel coronavirus disease of 2019 (COVID-19). Challenge 1 is about the SMEs' readiness or lack thereof, to innovate their business models. Challenge 2 concerns the SMEs' failure to embrace disruptive technology such as Intelligent Analytics (IA). The chapter looks into a systematic literature review, and surveys, and observes an infinite number of SMEs across northern Gauteng, South Africa. To a large extent, the systematic literature review focused on Asian SMEs. Though the chapter does not propose that the challenges facing SMEs are not unique to certain regions, there are instances wherein regions do matter. Therefore, the general feeling of the chapter is that the challenges identified can be better focused on South African SMEs.

---
[*] **Corresponding author Cecil Kgoetiane:** Department of Informatics, Faculty of ICT, Tshwane University of Technology, Pretoria, South Africa; Tel: +27 12 382-9093; E-mail: ckgoetiane@gmail.com

Ignitia Motjolopane, Ephias Ruhode and Pius Adewale Owolawi (Eds.)

For instance, the challenge of the SMEs' failure to embrace disruptive technology, such as Society 5.0, cannot be about Asian SMEs. The world has been evolving so much that Society 5.0 has become a global phenomenon sparking the interest of both society and government. From a social point of view, SMEs come to fulfill a role that will ultimately benefit both society and the government. The SMEs' failure to respond to challenges 1 and 2 makes it almost impossible for society to benefit from innovative services.

Hence, there is a wealth of opportunities for innovation within the Small and Medium Enterprise (SME) industry. A good starting point, therefore, will almost invariably be innovating the SMEs' business models. Simply riding on the wave of digital technology does not seem to unleash the full innovative potential of SMEs. Innovating business models and riding on the wave of digital technology (Muller, 2019); specifically IA, seems to work in favor of SMEs.

SMEs contribute to economic development (Pucihar, Lenart, Borštnar, Vidmar, and Marolt, 2019). Hence their business model innovation is the key to economic growth. In the same vein, big businesses stand to benefit from the SMEs' value proposition through an innovative business model. The world has gravitated toward digitalization and disruptive technologies for improved service and product offerings. On this basis, IA has been fulfilling this role of disruptive technology for obvious reasons.

METHODS AND DISCUSSION

In line with Xiao and Watson (2019), the chapter employed a systematic literature review. In so doing, two scholarly online databases, namely Google Scholar and Scopus, were searched to respond to whether the SMEs were ready to innovate their business models and subsequently embrace disruptive technology. A nonfinite sample of SMEs across northern Gauteng, South Africa, was surveyed and observed on their business model innovation readiness during and after the novel coronavirus disease of 2019 (COVID-19). Some SMEs went out of business at the height of the novel COVID-19 or reinvented themselves. Speaking of reinvention, this indicates that SMEs can innovate their business models when backed in a tight corner.

In the same breath, some new SMEs started during the peak of the novel COVID-19. Some of these SMEs simply rode on the wave of popular business, such as Personal Protective Equipment (PPE) and courier/delivery services. Most of these SMEs' businesses involved exports since the demand for PPE was ever rising across the globe.

With a confidence level of 95% and an expected error level (alpha) of 5%, the formula for the nonfinite sample size (raw) used was, therefore,

$$\tilde{n} = \left(\frac{\sigma^2 n}{s^2}\right)^{-\hat{E}}$$

Where $\tilde{n}$ was an estimated (raw) sample size.

With the novel COVID-19 unprecedented, there were some inconsistencies regarding some of the indexed literature findings concerning the SMEs' readiness to innovate their business models, and embrace disruptive technology. Pre-COVID-19, some findings were that the SMEs were not ready to innovate their business models (Ain *et al.*, 2019). By extension, the SMEs were not ready to take full advantage of disruptive technology for their smart operations.

Importantly, SMEs could hardly ever be ready to innovate their business models and embrace disruptive technology unless something drastic befell them. In this instance, the novel COVID-19 became an unexpected drastic measure that could not be ignored. Hence, post-COVID-19, there was a steady increase in the embrace of disruptive technology by SMEs toward innovating their business models.

OVERVIEW OF SMES AND THEIR IMPACT ON THE SOUTH AFRICAN ECONOMY

In line with Kgoetiane, Sibanda, and Mashau (2021), SMEs are the lifeblood of the economy. As such, SMEs contribute immensely toward job creation, economic development, and the country's Gross Domestic Product (GDP). Importantly, SMEs are the driving force behind innovation. Each country seems to have its own definition of SMEs. For instance, in the American context, an SME can consist of 1 to 500 employees. As far as South Africa is concerned, the Government Gazette (2003) and the South African National Small Business Act (1996:15-16) define an SME as follows:

A Small Enterprise is defined as an enterprise that consists of "less than 100 employees, formal and registered, has fixed business premises, and is owner-managed but has more complex management structure".

and

A Medium Enterprise is defined as an enterprise that consists of "up to 200 employees, still mainly owner-managed but consists of a decentralized management structure with the division of labor, and operates from fixed premises with formal requirements".

Understandably, with the onset of the coronavirus disease of 2019 (COVID-19), these definitions might need a revision of some sort. COVID-19 forced some SMEs to relook at their operating models. In the wake of the pandemic, some SMEs gave up their fixed premises in favor of virtual offices. The reasons for giving up fixed premises ranged from a cost containment perspective and riding on the wave of technology to embracing the metaverse age and Society 5.0.

Overview of Intelligent Analytics

In generic terms, analytics are used for predicting and understanding the future. Therefore, analytics in raw form can be categorized into four specific areas, namely, descriptive, diagnostic, predictive, and prescriptive. Each of these specific areas of analytics plays a given role as far as the future is concerned. Descriptive analytics is about understanding the past to predict the future. Diagnostic analytics is about delving deeper into the reasons that shaped the past. Predictive analytics rides on both descriptive and diagnostic analytics to better predict the future. Prescriptive analytics is about taking the necessary steps in preparation for the future.

Intelligent Analytics (IA) lends a great deal to taking the necessary steps or predictive analytics. The focus, therefore, shifts toward business optimization as predictive analytics entails more human input (even human-computer interface (HCI)), automated decision-making, and the resultant optimized action taken. All the same, it should be noted that it is only fair to highlight the notion that IA can be categorized into intelligent descriptive analytics, intelligent diagnostic analytics, intelligent predictive analytics, and intelligent prescriptive analytics (Fig. 1). From this it follows that IA integrates and taps into several key areas within data science. Amongst the key areas, IA is an integration of the basics, data, information, and knowledge (the centerpiece of Fig. 1). These basic areas can be summed up as intelligence and wisdom from a knowledge management point of view.

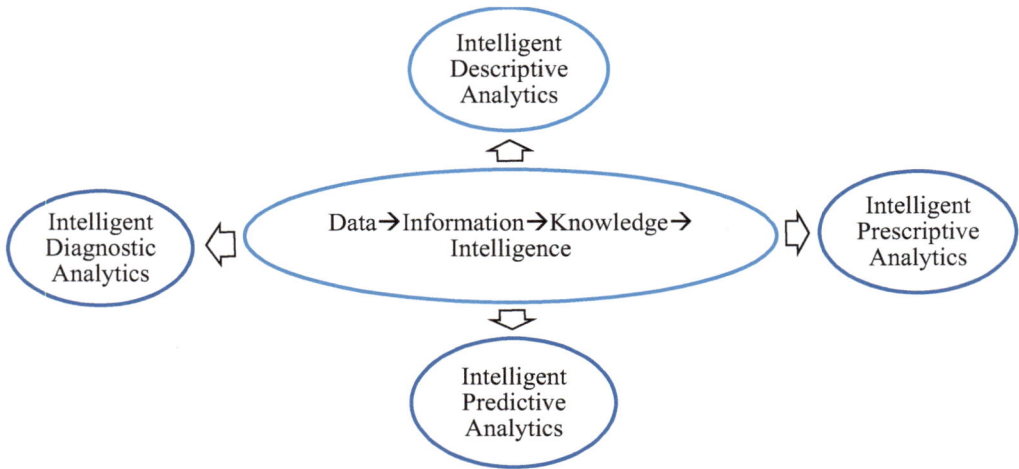

Fig. (1). Intelligent Analytics areas.

By definition, IA means gathering, organization, and analysis of big data. The integration, therefore, extends into the analytics of these basic areas. Artificial intelligence analytics, big data analytics, and other forms of analytics fall within the scope of the integration. In line with Sun (2021), IA is a form of disruptive technology in the sense that IA has been contributing immensely toward smarter ways of doing business. The smart ways of doing business range from areas such as SMEs, healthcare, and electronic commerce to financial services and global competitiveness, amongst others.

Society 5.0 and 4IR+ Leading into Intelligent Analytics

As the world evolves toward a re-imagined future, two concepts, namely Society 5.0 and the fourth industrial revolution plus (4IR+), invariably come to the fore. In its basic definition, Society 5.0 is a concept largely spearheaded by the East (Carraz and Harayama, 2019) that taps into disruptive technology to change and make society better. Making society better to some degree translates into innovation or the embrace thereof. As a concept, Society 5.0 is not some government-sponsored greenfield project. Neither can Society 5.0 be some sort of a brownfield project. Rather, Society 5.0 calls for a concerted effort from all social quarters for the betterment of society.

On the other hand, 4IR+ is about technological advances in such areas as data science, big data analytics, Intelligent Analytics, artificial intelligence, robotics and machine learning, the Internet of Things (IoT), etc. Therefore, there cannot be Society 5.0 without 4IR+. Otherwise, the two concepts need each other so society can ultimately take advantage of either or both. Importantly, the two concepts are about innovation. SMEs are either the center or at the center of innovation, depending on how society looks at the SMEs.

Ergo, as far as the innovation of SMEs in their entirety goes, the said concepts stand out. Society 5.0 and the fourth industrial revolution plus (4IR+) account for a significant part of innovation. In the first place, the evolution of Society 4.0 to the current Society 5.0 envisioned an economy largely driven by innovative approaches rather than financial might. In the same vein, SMEs exist for various reasons, including pacesetters for innovation and contribution to the economy. Therefore, from the perspective of Society 5.0, access to financial might should not stand in the way of the SMEs' innovative approaches. In line with Hamdani, Herlianti, and Amin (2019), the integration of humans with machines or technology should therefore be taking priority over access to capital.

Such integration is conditional upon the availability of big data and the harnessing thereof. Importantly, the focus in this instance shifts toward intelligent analytics, an aspect of the 4IR+. Integrating humans with technology, or Intelligent analytics (IA) specifically, for socio-economic development indicates that innovation should not be about capital but rather about access to data (Qu, Shi, Zhao, Yu, and Yu, 2021). In the same breath, innovation comes naturally when SMEs integrate IA with their business model designs. For SMEs, integrating IA with their business model designs (Qu *et al.*, 2021; Gatautis, Vaiciukynaite, and Tarute, 2019) seems the best bet in terms of innovation and further unlocking Society 5.0 opportunities.

While SMEs exist for various reasons, including creating and sustaining jobs and creating new lines of business (Kgoetiane *et al.*, 2021), they are also responsible for wealth creation as well. Effectively, all the said initiatives by the SMEs tend to ride on the wave of Society 5.0 for obvious reasons. An improved society is aimed at improved socio-economic development and the betterment of the world. The literature (*inter alia* Holroyd, 2022) may claim certain victories about Society 5.0 in certain regions of the world, particularly the Far East and the New World, the Americas. Despite this claim, the SME environment across the world has been evolving at such great speed that SMEs collectively owe their small victories to digital innovation.

The evolution of the SME environment has been triggered by Society 5.0, 4IR+, and, lately, the advent of the novel coronavirus disease of 2019 (COVID-19). The SMEs take the initiative for innovative ways while governments fund such innovation initiatives. Therefore, unlocking innovative approaches and opportunities seems to have little to do with the financial strength of the SMEs but rather access to government-led funding, public-private partnerships (PPP), or any other funding originating from other quarters. However, Holroyd (2022) laments the fact that where the government is involved, processes tend to be laborious and unimaginably slow. This is the case since most of these innovative initiatives carry an element of risk. As such, investing government funds in risky initiatives needs to be well calculated. As far as the PPP initiatives go, there is always a question of poor appetite between the public and private sectors due to poor trust issues between the two sectors.

On the other hand, it is to be expected that where the competition is stiff, as is the case within the SME game, it is only fair that every effort taken should result in value for money. That is, all monies distributed should bear a good return on investment. Despite all this slowness in action attributed to the government, Society 5.0 has rolled on. As such, the SMEs cannot help but embrace Society 5.0 and make it evolve further, at least at the rate at which the integration of technology and socio-economic development is going. By the same measure, 4IR+ relies on everything digital. The digitalization of processes, for instance, ties well with integrating technology and socio-economic development.

From the perspective of SMEs, 4IR+ contributes immensely to innovation. On this basis, it becomes practicable for the SMEs to successfully execute the greenfield projects they typically initiate to contribute to socio-economic development. In the same vein, the government entrusts the SMEs with its brownfield initiatives, such as inner city and infrastructural development projects, *inter alia*. Importantly, innovation counts on a great number of factors. Unlocking innovation, therefore, begins with innovating the SMEs' business models by employing such approaches as IA. This digital approach follows on the coattails of 4IR+ and other accompanying emerging and disruptive technologies that fall outside of the scope of this chapter.

How COVID-19 Accelerated the Adoption of Disruptive Technology?

Thus, Intelligent Analytics (IA) has been at the forefront of digital innovation for quite some time now. Yet, with the advent of the novel coronavirus disease of 2019 (COVID-19), the significance of IA to digital innovation has been steadily increasing (Ahmad and Miskon, 2020; Carroll and Conboy, 2020), particularly within the SMEs' space. For various reasons, SMEs need to embrace IA not only to aid in innovating their business models but for overall survival and long-run sustainability. Such embrace of IA is critical to better participate in the global competitive SME environment (Salisu, Bin Mohd Sappri, and Bin Omar, 2021), where threats and opportunities must be exploited.

From the point of view of threats and opportunities, IA comes into its own for the appraisal (Combita Niño, Cómbita Niño, and Morales Ortega, 2020; Harrison, Parker, Brosas, Chiong, and Tian, 2015) and subsequent appreciation of these factors. Admittedly, as COVID-19 wrought great havoc across the SME space through the threats that made some SMEs take a bath or even fold business, so did COVID-19 bring many opportunities in its wake. One aspect, in terms of the opportunities, is the discovery of knowledge (Ain, Vaia, DeLone, and Waheed, 2019), reuse, and harnessing thereof. Knowledge discovery has been a key aspect as far as SMEs' sustainability goes. This aspect deals with such issues as process digitalization, knowledge transfer, and business continuity.

Importantly, besides big data, knowledge discovery forms the basis of IA, wherein the SMEs need to perform data analysis for subsequent trend analysis and better decision-making. This, therefore, enables the SMEs to respond better to threats while at the same time taking advantage of the opportunities. On the other hand, big data have seen big strides over the years such that SMEs' smart decision-making has come to benefit from digital innovation (Cheng, Zhong, and Cao, 2020; Ain *et al.*, 2019; Arnott, Lizama, and Song, 2017) to a large degree.

SMEs' Business Model Innovation

Regardless of an SME's relative size, taking full advantage of Industry 4.0 and an innovative business model, an SME ought to look at the whole value creation concept from two viewpoints (Kagermann, Wahlster, and Helbig, 2013). That is, the SME needs to look at itself as both the provider and beneficiary or, rather, as the recipient of an innovative business model. It needs to be pointed out that most SMEs that fall within the small enterprise category tend to face challenges with innovation, probably due to insufficient access to resources (Kgoetiane *et al.*, 2021). To some degree, the size of an SME seems to arguably affect the SMEs' innovation drive (Welmilla, Weerakkody, and Ediriweera 2011).

On a different note, innovating the SMEs' business models makes them respond better to unforeseen and emerging challenges such as the recent global COVID-19 pandemic. For instance, during the peak of COVID-19, most SMEs faced great challenges (Gibson, 2020) to the point of folding business. Typically, SMEs do not benefit from government relief (Giones, Brem, Pollack, Michaelis, Klyver, and Brinckmann, 2020), though, at the peak of COVID-19, governments offered some paltry relief to the SMEs.

As such, some SMEs were forced to innovate their business models in response to the pandemic though some failed dismally as this was too short a notice for them to innovate. Hence, some had to, unfortunately, close shop completely, as alluded to earlier. Besides forcing some SMEs out of business, the pandemic introduced some dichotomies in consumer choices and generic responses toward some of the services offered by the SMEs (Bivona and Cruz, 2020).

By their nature, SMEs are comparatively more affected by crises than big businesses (Mayr, Mitter, and Aichmayr, 2017; Herbane, 2013). This is the case since the volatility index is somewhat higher within SMEs than it is the case with big businesses. As a consequence, innovating the business models helps SMEs better perform environmental scans from the perspective of the Threats, Opportunities, Weaknesses, and Strengths (TOWS) analysis. Similarly, such innovation helps SMEs prepare better for crises. In any event, every business, by expectation, is supposed to imagine its business model in terms of uncertainty (Liu, Lee, and Lee, 2020), as such, take advantage of such models as the TOWS to prepare for uncertain times.

The economic world has evolved to the so-called Industry 4.0. In the same sort, the digital world has evolved to the so-called 4IR+. Given these developments, the metaverse has somehow taken over the day-to-day SMEs' activities. SMEs play a lead role as far as the metaverse is concerned. Importantly, such a lead role becomes possible through the SMEs' business model innovation (BMI).

From an Industry 4.0 perspective, SMEs become innovative only when their business models have been innovated (Baden-Fuller and Haefliger, 2013). By extension, innovating business models equate to adopting and embracing technology, be it disruptive technology such as Intelligent Analytics, to create, deliver, and capture value (Teece, 2010) to the SMEs' customer base. Depending on which product lines or service offerings the SMEs are into, the value they create for their customer base needs to innovate in line with Industry 4.0 (Müller, Buliga, and Voigt, 2018; Ehret and Wirtz, 2017; Arnold, Kiel, and Voigt, 2016). On more scores than one, the basis of the SMEs' BMI is a disruptive technology. The real reason in this instance is that the SMEs are the driving force behind innovation (Baden-Fuller and Haefliger, 2013) at the time, contributing toward innovative initiatives in the bigger businesses as well.

SMEs' Business Model Innovation Readiness

With so much global interest in Intelligent Analytics (IA) (Trieu, 2017), SMEs are yet to fully embrace IA (Sayyed-Alikhani, Chica, and Mohammadi, 2021; Behl, Dutta, Lessmann, Dwivedi, and Kar, 2019) with the view to innovating their business models. The SMEs' embrace of IA is yet to improve, as Ain *et al.* (2019) found out. It is invariably challenging to measure the SMEs' business model innovation (BMI) readiness (Magaireah, Sulaiman, and Ali, 2019), given that several factors go into the basket of the SMEs' BMI. For instance, with IA being just one of those factors, SMEs have so far been slow in embracing digital innovation. This, in turn, impacts the benefits to be realized from the SMEs' BMI. In the same breath, it is a question of whether the SMEs find IA, or the embrace thereof, pertinent to their space, inclusive of helping the SMEs remain sustainable in the long run.

What makes the situation even more challenging is the fact that some of these SMEs do not necessarily keep themselves abreast of the latest happenings concerning technology. This may be put down to the SMEs' owner-managers' appreciation of technology and the application thereof for growth and sustainability. Therefore, what the extant literature has found to be wanting about the SMEs' readiness to innovate their business models (Ain *et al.*, 2019) may be worse even. For instance, BMI is supposed to aid SMEs ride on the wave of technology to improve (Sheng, Amankwah-Amoah, Khan, and Wang, 2020; van Rijmenam, Erekhinskaya, Schweitzer, and Williams, 2019) their overall way of doing business. At the same time, SMEs are expected to realize sustainability as they work smarter and grow.

However, from the growth and sustainability point of view, it invariably boils down to a specific SME (Salisu *et al.*, 2021) embracing an innovative business model. The SMEs have various options available to them, such as initiating technological development partnerships with their peers, including big businesses and sponsoring graduate programs, amongst others. These options present several opportunities from a BMI point of view. Admittedly, what makes or breaks an SME is the business model. The success of everything else will then be conditional upon the innovative business model. The drivers behind these business models are the SMEs' owner-managers.

Implications of Business Model Innovation

Looking at some of the literature concerning the low-hanging fruits of innovating SMEs' business models leaves some questions unanswered. Innovation may not necessarily be the silver bullet for the plethora of issues that SMEs face in their lifetime. For instance, some of the literature questions the implication of innovating the SMEs' business models (Presenza and Petruzzelli, 2019; Foss and Saebi, 2018; Franceschelli, Sandoro, and Candelo, 2018; Futterer, Schmidt, and Heidenreich, 2018) to better deal with crises. Just how does business model innovation (BMI) help prepare SMEs for dealing with a crisis such as COVID-19? This concern is justified, particularly when the SMEs' approach to innovation is misguided.

To begin with, business model innovation (BMI) should be approached from a digital perspective. Importantly, Intelligent Analytics (IA), as alluded to earlier, is about revolutionizing the SMEs' business models toward better dealing with both uncertainty and crises. The other approach that supports BMI is embracing sector-level collaboration (Dezi, Ferraris, Papa, and Vrontis, 2021; Ferraris, Vrontis, Belyaeva, De Bernardi, and Ozek, 2020; Wang and Kimble, 2016) inclusive of sharing intelligence with stakeholders on a regular basis. Importantly, the sector-level collaboration is seen as a symbiotic arrangement geared toward benefiting all role players in BMI. Given the government's poor appetite for the PPP wherein the SMEs are especially involved, the SMEs cannot afford to fail in innovating their business models. Further, IA exposes SMEs to emerging and disruptive technologies aimed at improving the whole approach to BMI for better service delivery.

The Role of the SMEs' Owner-managers

An SME's owner-manager is an entrepreneur who starts up an SME and goes on to manage such an SME. The owner-manager can hire a manager or managers depending on the extent of the responsibilities to be discharged within the SME. In this case, these managers are referred to as employed managers. The distinction of the roles may not necessarily matter until such big decisions as innovation come into play. Therefore, the role of the SMEs' owner-managers is critical in the ultimate innovation of the SMEs' business models. To a large degree, the SMEs' owner-managers' inherent skills and exposure to intelligent analytics (IA) (Liang and Liu, 2018; Sun, Cegielski, Jia, and Hall, 2018) play a lead role in embracing digital innovation. Conversely, the lack of skills and exposure to IA limits the SMEs from taking advantage of digital innovation, thereby scarcely innovating their SMEs' business models. By extension, the SMEs' stakeholders' lack of exposure to IA limits the scope of innovating the SMEs' business models.

The SMEs' owner-managers' exposure to expertise in IA, even big data analytics, makes it easy for them to embrace (Mosweu, Bwalya, and Mutshewa, 2016) and take advantage of an innovative business model. By the same token, such exposure to IA, even big data analytics by the SMEs' owner-managers or the SMEs' stakeholders makes technology appraisal doable by the SMEs (Gruenhagen and Parker, 2020; Hawash, Mokhtar, Yusof, and Mukred, 2020; Mukred, Yusof, Mokhtar, and Fauzi, 2019; Mosweu *et al.*, 2016).

The technology appraisal might lead to the embrace thereof. Therefore, the SMEs and their owner-managers/stakeholders must understand several Information Systems (IS) theories that can, in turn, make it easy to embrace technology ultimately. For instance, at the SME level, theories such as Diffusion of Innovation (DOI), institutional theory, Resource-Based View (RBV), and Technology Organization Environment (TOE) (Salisu *et al.*, 2021) are applicable. On the other hand, at the SMEs' owner-managers/stakeholders level, such theories as the unified theory of acceptance and use of technology (UTAUT), theory of planned behavior (TPB), and IS adoption model (Salisu *et al.*, 2021) are applicable.

From a theoretical point of view, Rogers' (2003) DOI seems the best bet as far as the understanding of the technology is concerned (Banapour *et al.*, 2020; Khayer, Talukder, Bao, and Hossain, 2020; Ma and Lee, 2019). However, it would not be such a bad idea to look into the TOE theory, given its inherent strengths. For instance, the overall innovation within the SMEs' environment or space could somehow trigger the embrace of technological innovation in a particular SME.

When all is said and done, the SMEs' owner-managers do not have to grasp the finer details of the different models highlighted earlier. What should be key is that the SMEs' owner-managers only need to understand how to apply the models as such benefit from their application. This can be done in association with the key staffers within the SME. In any event, these key SME staffers' role is to bridge the gap between the owner-managers and modeling.

CONCLUDING REMARKS

The chapter highlighted two challenges regarding SMEs in the South African context. The first challenge was about the SMEs' readiness, or lack thereof, to innovate their business models. The second challenge was the SMEs' failure to embrace disruptive technology such as Intelligent Analytics (IA). To find solutions to the challenges highlighted, the chapter looked into a systematic literature review and surveyed and observed an infinite number of SMEs across northern Gauteng, South Africa. Admittedly, the literature review focused on Asian SMEs to a larger degree.

In the final analysis, innovating the SMEs' business models favors the SMEs' growth (Cosenz and Bivona, 2020) and sustainability in the long run. For instance, sustainability is conditional upon the constant demand for the service and/or product offerings of the SMEs by their customer base. Such sustained demand for the SMEs' services and/or products depends on meeting the customer base's innovative needs. The customer base will always look for something innovative that ticks their boxes. At the same time, it puts all sorts of pressure on SMEs. Therefore, understanding such pressures and preempting them to a certain degree will come in handy. In the same breath, Intelligent Analytics seems to work in favor of the SMEs while responding to the pressures to which the customer base subjects the SMEs in the name of innovation.

GLOSSARY

Business model.	In the business strategy context, the business model outlines how an SME will create, deliver, and capture value for its customers.
Business Model Innovation.	The modification of an SME's business model to improve value creation through the embrace of digital technology.
Disruptive Technology.	Innovation that largely changes the way SMEs operate and create value. Disruptive technology works hand in hand with [and relies on] business model innovation.
Industry 4.0.	The rapid technological transformation that embraces Society 5.0.
Intelligent Analytics.	The gathering organization, and analysis of big data. Intelligent Analytics integrates and employs numerous key areas in the data science context.
Operating model.	It is an extension of the business model. The operating model visualizes the business model for both the SME employees and its customers.
Owner-manager.	An SME owner who also manages the SME.
Predictive analytics.	Uses descriptive and diagnostic analytics to better predict the future. Predictive analytics is about SME optimization.
Public-private partnership.	In the South African context, a Public-private partnership (PPP) is a contractual partnership entered into between the public-sector and private-sector partners where the majority of the risk is transferred to the private-sector partners. In terms of the PPP, the private-sector partner is granted the right to use government property and perform some functions that would usually be fulfilled by the government.
Society 5.0.	A concept that taps into disruptive technology to change and make society better through the integration of cyber- and physical spaces.

REFERENCES

Ahmad, S & Miskon, S (2020) The adoption of business intelligence systems in textile and apparel industry: Case studies. In: Saeed, F., Gazem, N., (Eds.), *Emerging Trends in Intelligent Computing and Informatics* Springer Nature, Switzerland AG 12-23.
[http://dx.doi.org/10.1007/978-3-030-33582-3_2]

Ain, N, Vaia, G, DeLone, WH & Waheed, M (2019) Two decades of research on business intelligence system adoption, utilization and success – A systematic literature review. *Decis Support Syst,* 125, 113113.
[http://dx.doi.org/10.1016/j.dss.2019.113113]

Arnold, C, Kiel, D & Voigt, KI (2016) How the industrial internet of things changes business models in different manufacturing industries. *Int J Innov Manage,* 20, 1640015.
[http://dx.doi.org/10.1142/S1363919616400156]

Arnott, D, Lizama, F & Song, Y (2017) Patterns of business intelligence systems use in organizations. *Decis Support Syst,* 97, 58-68.
[http://dx.doi.org/10.1016/j.dss.2017.03.005]

Baden-Fuller, C & Haefliger, S (2013) Business models and technological innovation. *Long Range Plann,* 46, 419-26.

[http://dx.doi.org/10.1016/j.lrp.2013.08.023]

Banapour, P, Yuh, B, Chenam, A, Shen, JK, Ruel, N, Han, ES, Kim, JY, Maghami, EG, Pigazzi, A, Raz, DJ, Singh, GP, Wakabayashi, M, Woo, Y, Fong, Y & Lau, CS (2021) Readmission and complications after robotic surgery: Experience of 10,000 operations at a comprehensive cancer center. *J Robot Surg,* 15, 37-44. [http://dx.doi.org/10.1007/s11701-020-01077-4] [PMID: 32277400]

Behl, A, Dutta, P, Lessmann, S, Dwivedi, YK & Kar, S (2019) A conceptual framework for the adoption of big data analytics by e-commerce startups: A case-based approach. *Inf Syst E-Bus Manag,* 17, 285-318. [http://dx.doi.org/10.1007/s10257-019-00452-5]

Carraz, R & Harayama, Y (2019) Japan's innovation system at a crossroads: Society 5.0. In: Echle, C., (Ed.),*Digital Asia (Panorama: Insights into European and Asian Affairs), Konrad-Adenauer-Stiftung Ltd* 39–40.

Carroll, N & Conboy, K (2020) Normalising the "new normal": Changing tech-driven work practices under pandemic time pressure. *Int J Inf Manage,* 55, 102186. [http://dx.doi.org/10.1016/j.ijinfomgt.2020.102186] [PMID: 32836643]

Cheng, C, Zhong, H & Cao, L (2020) Facilitating speed of internationalization: The roles of business intelligence and organizational agility. *J Bus Res,* 110, 95-103. [http://dx.doi.org/10.1016/j.jbusres.2020.01.003]

Combita Niño, H A, Cómbita Niño, J P & Morales Ortega, R (2020) Business intelligence governance framework in a university: Universidad de la costa case study. *International Journal of Information Management,* 50, 405-12. [http://dx.doi.org/10.1016/j.ijinfomgt.2018.11.012]

Cosenz, F & Bivona, E (2021) Fostering growth patterns of SMEs through business model innovation. A tailored dynamic business modelling approach. *J Bus Res,* 130, 658-69. [http://dx.doi.org/10.1016/j.jbusres.2020.03.003]

Dezi, L, Ferraris, A, Papa, A & Vrontis, D (2021) The role of external embeddedness and knowledge management as antecedents of ambidexterity and performances in Italian SMEs. *IEEE Transactions on Engineering Management,* 68, 360-9. [http://dx.doi.org/10.1109/TEM.2019.2916378]

Ehret, M & Wirtz, J (2017) Unlocking value from machines: Business models and the industrial internet of things. *J Mark Manage,* 33, 111-30. [http://dx.doi.org/10.1080/0267257X.2016.1248041]

Ferraris, A, Vrontis, D, Belyaeva, Z, De Bernardi, P & Ozek, H (2020) Innovation within the food companies: How creative partnerships may conduct to better performances? *Br Food J,* 123, 143-58. [http://dx.doi.org/10.1108/BFJ-07-2019-0502]

Foss, NJ & Saebi, T (2018) Business models and business model innovation: Between wicked and paradigmatic problems. *Long Range Plann,* 51, 9-21. [http://dx.doi.org/10.1016/j.lrp.2017.07.006]

Franceschelli, MV, Santoro, G & Candelo, E (2018) Business model innovation for sustainability: A food start-up case study. *Br Food J,* 120, 2483-94. [http://dx.doi.org/10.1108/BFJ-01-2018-0049]

Futterer, F, Schmidt, J & Heidenreich, S (2018) Effectuation or causation as the key to corporate venture success? Investigating effects of entrepreneurial behaviors on business model innovation and venture performance. *Long Range Plann,* 51, 64-81. [http://dx.doi.org/10.1016/j.lrp.2017.06.008]

Gatautis, R, Vaiciukynaite, E & Tarute, A (2019) Impact of business model innovations on SME's innovativeness and performance. *Balt J Manag,* 14, 521-39. [http://dx.doi.org/10.1108/BJM-01-2018-0035]

Gibson, C (2020) From 'social distancing' to 'care in connecting': An emerging organizational research

agenda for turbulent times. *Acad Manag Discov,* 6, 165-9.
[http://dx.doi.org/10.5465/amd.2020.0062]

Giones, F, Brem, A, Pollack, JM, Michaelis, TL, Klyver, K & Brinckmann, J (2020) Revising entrepreneurial action in response to exogenous shocks: Considering the COVID-19 pandemic. *Journal of Business Venturing Insights,* 14, e00186.
[http://dx.doi.org/10.1016/j.jbvi.2020.e00186]

Government Gazette of the Republic of South Africa (2003) *National Small Business Amendment Act* Available from: http//www.info.gov.za/gazette/acts/2003/a26-03/pdf (Accessed on 16 Sep 2022).

Gruenhagen, JH & Parker, R (2020) Factors driving or impeding the diffusion and adoption of innovation in mining: A systematic review of the literature. *Resour Policy,* 65, 101540.
[http://dx.doi.org/10.1016/j.resourpol.2019.101540]

Harrison, R, Parker, A, Brosas, G, Chiong, R & Tian, X (2015) The role of technology in the management and exploitation of internal business intelligence. *J Syst Inf Technol,* 17, 247-62.
[http://dx.doi.org/10.1108/JSIT-04-2015-0030]

Hawash, B, Mokhtar, UA, Yusof, ZM & Mukred, M (2020) The adoption of electronic records management system (ERMS) in the Yemeni oil and gas sector. *Rec Manage J,* 30, 1-22.
[http://dx.doi.org/10.1108/RMJ-03-2019-0010]

Herbane, B (2013) Exploring crisis management in UK small- and medium-sized enterprises. *J Contingencies Crisis Manage,* 21, 82-95.
[http://dx.doi.org/10.1111/1468-5973.12006]

Hlophego Kgoetiane, C, Sibanda, R & Mashau, P (2021) The Effect of the Competitive Strategies on the Tshwane-based SMEs' Performance. *African Journal of Business and Economic Research,* 16, 223-43.
[http://dx.doi.org/10.31920/1750-4562/2021/v16n2a11]

Kagermann, H, Wahlster, W & Helbig, J (2013) *Recommendations for implementing the strategic initiative Industrie 40 – final report of the Industrie 40 working group.* Communication Promoters Group of the Industry-Science Research, Frankfurt.

Khayer, A, Talukder, MS, Bao, Y & Hossain, MN (2020) Cloud computing adoption and its impact on SMEs' performance for cloud supported operations: A dual-stage analytical approach. *Technol Soc,* 60, 101225.
[http://dx.doi.org/10.1016/j.techsoc.2019.101225]

Liu, Y, Lee, JM & Lee, C (2020) The challenges and opportunities of a global health crisis: The management and business implications of COVID-19 from an Asian perspective. *Asian Bus Manage,* 19, 277-97.
[http://dx.doi.org/10.1057/s41291-020-00119-x]

Louangrath, PI (2014) Sample size determination for non-finite population. *International Conference on Discrete Mathematics and Applied Science.*

Ma, L & Lee, CS (2019) Investigating the adoption of MOOC s: A technology–user–environment perspective. *J Comput Assist Learn,* 35, 89-98.
[http://dx.doi.org/10.1111/jcal.12314]

Magaireah, AI, Sulaiman, H & Ali, N (2019) Identifying the most critical factors to business intelligence implementation success in the public sector organizations. *Journal of Social Sciences Research,* 5, 450-62.
[http://dx.doi.org/10.32861/jssr.52.450.462]

Mayr, S, Mitter, C & Aichmayr, A (2017) Corporate crisis and sustainable reorganization: evidence from bankrupt Austrian SMEs. *J Small Bus Manag,* 55, 108-27.
[http://dx.doi.org/10.1111/jsbm.12248]

Mosweu, O, Bwalya, K & Mutshewa, A (2016) Examining factors affecting the adoption and usage of document workflow management system (DWMS) using the UTAUT model. *Rec Manage J,* 26, 38-67.
[http://dx.doi.org/10.1108/RMJ-03-2015-0012]

Mukred, M, Yusof, ZM, Mokhtar, UA & Fauzi, F (2019) Taxonomic framework for factors influencing ERMS adoption in organisations of higher professional education. *J Inf Sci,* 45, 139-55.
[http://dx.doi.org/10.1177/0165551518783133]

Müller, JM (2019) Business model innovation in small- and medium-sized enterprises. *J Manuf Tech Manag,* 30, 1127-42.
[http://dx.doi.org/10.1108/JMTM-01-2018-0008]

Müller, JM & Voigt, KI (2018) Sustainable industrial value creation in SMEs: A comparison between industry 4.0 and Made in China 2025. *International Journal of Precision Engineering and Manufacturing – Green Technology,* 5, 659-70.
[http://dx.doi.org/10.1007/s40684-018-0056-z]

National Small Business Act. *President's Office, Pretoria, South Africa.*
[http://dx.doi.org/10.1016/j.ijhm.2019.03.027]

Presenza, A & Messeni Petruzzelli, A (2019) Investigating business model innovation in Haute Cuisine. Role and behavior of chef-entrepreneurs. *Int J Hospit Manag,* 82, 101-11.
[http://dx.doi.org/10.1016/j.ijhm.2019.03.027]

Pucihar, A, Lenart, G, Kljajić Borštnar, M, Vidmar, D & Marolt, M (2019) Drivers and outcomes of business model innovation—micro, small and medium-sized enterprises perspective. *Sustainability,* 11, 344.
[http://dx.doi.org/10.3390/su11020344]

Rogers, EM (2003) *Diffusion of Innovation* The Free Press.

Salisu, I, Bin Mohd Sappri, M & Bin Omar, MF (2021) The adoption of business intelligence systems in small and medium enterprises in the healthcare sector: A systematic literature review. *Cogent Business & Management,* 8, 1935663.
[http://dx.doi.org/10.1080/23311975.2021.1935663]

Sayyed-Alikhani, A, Chica, M & Mohammadi, A (2021) An agent-based system for modeling users' acquisition and retention in startup apps. *Expert Syst Appl,* 176, 114861.
[http://dx.doi.org/10.1016/j.eswa.2021.114861]

Sheng, J, Amankwah-Amoah, J, Khan, Z & Wang, X (2020) COVID-19 pandemic in the new era of big data analytics: Methodological innovations and future research directions. *Br J Manage,* 1-20.

Sun, Z (2021) "An Introduction to Intelligent Analytics," PNG UoT BAIS.6, 1-6.
[http://dx.doi.org/10.13140/RG.2.2.32783.71843]

Sun, S, Cegielski, CG, Jia, L & Hall, DJ (2018) Understanding the factors affecting the organizational adoption of big data. *J Comput Inf Syst,* 58, 193-203.
[http://dx.doi.org/10.1080/08874417.2016.1222891]

Teece, DJ (2010) Business models, business strategy and innovation. *Long Range Plann,* 43, 172-94.
[http://dx.doi.org/10.1016/j.lrp.2009.07.003]

Trieu, VH (2017) Getting value from Business Intelligence systems: A review and research agenda. *Decis Support Syst,* 93, 111-24.
[http://dx.doi.org/10.1016/j.dss.2016.09.019]

van Rijmenam, M, Erekhinskaya, T, Schweitzer, J & Williams, MA (2019) Avoid being the Turkey: How big data analytics changes the game of strategy in times of ambiguity and uncertainty. *Long Range Planning,* 52, 101-841.
[http://dx.doi.org/10.1016/j.lrp.2018.05.007]

Wang, H & Kimble, C (2016) How external factors influence business model innovation: A study of the Bosch Group and the Chinese automotive aftermarket. *Glob Bus Organ Excell,* 35, 53-64.
[http://dx.doi.org/10.1002/joe.21712]

Welmilla, I, Weerakkody, WAS & Ediriweera, AN (2011) *The Impact of Demographic Factors of Entrepreneurs on Development of SMEs in Tourism Industry in Sri Lanka, Faculty of Commerce and*

Management Studies. University of Kelaniya, Sri Lanka.

Xiao, Y & Watson, M (2019) Guidance on conducting a systematic literature review. *J Plann Educ Res,* 39, 93-112.
[http://dx.doi.org/10.1177/0739456X17723971]

Digital Transformation in SMEs: Developing Digital Business Model Innovations Based on Artificial Intelligence

Tlou Maggie Masenya[1,*]

[1] *Durban University of Technology, Berea, South Africa*

Abstract: The strategic goal of most organisations is to improve business operations for successful organisational performance. Digital transformation is a time of swift technological changes posing an ongoing challenge for Small and Medium Enterprises (SMEs) to establish high-performance work systems for organisational performance. Hence SMEs are exploring new technologies to stay competitive and develop innovative business models in the digital transformation era. Artificial Intelligence (AI) technologies may enable SMEs to enhance practices and improve their business model innovation strategies. This chapter examined the existing literature on the digital transformation of SMEs by implementing Artificial Intelligence. The goal was to emphasise how AI can significantly change business processes, practices, and overall organisational performance, ultimately supporting the development of digital business models in SMEs. The study's findings indicated that AI holds great potential for SMEs to enhance their business processes, practices, and overall performance, enabling them to better navigate their increasingly competitive environment. Therefore, it is recommended that managers of SMEs explore opportunities to incorporate AI and other advanced technologies into their business innovation processes. By doing so, SMEs can generate tangible value by strengthening their dynamic capabilities, improving efficiency, and mitigating operational risks.

Keywords: Artificial Intelligence, Business model innovation, Digital technologies, Digital transformation, Small and Medium-sized Enterprises.

INTRODUCTION

Digital transformation poses challenges for small and medium enterprises (SMEs) as digital transformation is drastically reshaping the business environment and creating new opportunities through integrating information, communication, and emerging connectivity technologies (Bharadwaj *et al.*, 2013). The emerging disruptive technologies include artificial intelligence, the Internet of Things, and

---

[*] **Corresponding author Tlou Maggie Masenya:** Durban University of Technology, Berea, South Africa, South Africa; E-mail: tloum@dut.ac.za

Ignitia Motjolopane, Ephias Ruhode and Pius Adewale Owolawi (Eds.)

big data analytics, to name a few (Teffo, Motjolopane & Masenya, 2022). Globally, SMEs are increasingly adopting these innovative technologies to enhance business practices, improve business performance, deliver brand services, and develop new business innovation strategies. This technology-driven era is thus revolutionising SMEs globally and is an entrepreneurial process whereby SMEs are developing digital business models. Therefore, the digital transformation era is vital for SMEs to innovate and compete (Akpan, Soopramanien & Kwak, 2020). According to Peter, *et al*, (2019), the digital transformation's continuous interplay between business and technology has become incredibly clear as companies adapt to the new possibilities and difficulties by strategically digitising business operations. Digital transformation enhances efficiency throughout the value chain through technology, as stated by Stich and Hering (2015). Furthermore, as highlighted by Fettke, *et al*, (2014), each significant shift in industrial revolutions is accompanied by the introduction of novel technologies. Adapting and reshaping traditional business strategies with emerging new technologies is necessary in the digital transformation context. According to Peter *et al*. (2019), digital transformation requires SMEs to embrace and implement digital technologies such as business processes and practices. Thus, disruptive technologies such as big data analytics, Artificial Intelligence, and the Internet of Things radically shift how SMEs create and deliver customer value. In the digital transformation context, adapting and reshaping traditional business strategies with emerging new technologies is necessary. Integrating emerging technologies may lead to profound changes in value creation and business model innovation (Garzella, *et al*, 2021).

Wang, *et al*, (2022) describe business innovation as an organisation incorporating new procedures and services to influence the business positively. In addition, Vils *et al*. (2017) define business model innovation as the process by which companies create and acquire value through the organisation of internal processes and external relationships with customers and suppliers. Business model innovation may be linked to intelligent analytics in the digital transformation era. Sun and Stranieri (2021) described smart analytics as science and technology about collecting, organising and analysing big data to discover and visualise patterns through artificial intelligence systems.

As such, the impact of digital transformation and digitalisation demonstrates that digital technologies and intelligent analytics can no longer be regarded merely as a subordinate support function but as an integral part of the business and enterprises (El Sawy & Pereira, 2013).

PROBLEM STATEMENT

In a business environment facing digital transformation, SMEs face mounting pressure to maintain competitiveness, relevance and significance in society (Organization for Economic Co-operation and Development, 2017). Moreover, this underscores a need to adopt emerging digital technologies. However, SMEs face challenges in embracing emerging technologies from limited skills and funds and the lack of knowledge necessary to effectively utilise these advanced technologies without suitable business models for digital transformation. Hence Linde, *et al*, (2021) and Trischler and Li-Ying (2023) suggest that digital transformation often needs to catch up in numerous companies failing to realise the potential benefits of significant investments in emerging technologies. Furthermore, Travaly and Muvunyi (2020) indicate that a lack of relevant technical skills among young people is one of the significant threats and barriers to realising emerging technologies' full potential.

SMEs are more inclined to transform their existing business models, including their prime objectives and approaches to value creation. SMEs may benefit from the wealth of new technologies by basing their business models on artificial intelligent technologies, which creatively use existing services and protocols to develop more responsive and dynamic products. Artificial Intelligence can communicate directly with the user or other machines to offer a brand-new level of interaction in any environment. Therefore, in a digital transformation era, adopting emerging technologies such as Artificial Intelligence is a pressing need to support digital business models. To stay competitive within the dynamic and demanding digital business landscape, SMEs must focus on designing and developing digital business models (Schoemaker *et al.*, 2018). This chapter thus examined the adoption of Artificial Intelligence for digital business model innovation in SMEs as a response to digital transformation.

OBJECTIVES

The research objectives which underpinned this chapter were to:

• Determine the impact of digital transformation on business processes and practices in SMEs.

• Determine the strategies for effective development of business model innovation within SMEs.

• Determine the adoption of Artificial Intelligence as a driver for business innovation models in SMEs.

• Propose a Digital Business Model Innovation framework applicable to SMEs.

CONCEPTUAL FRAMEWORK

Business model components are essential elements that significantly impact the performance of both SMEs and large businesses (Ramdani *et al.*, 2019). Therefore, they are crucial in driving business model innovation within South African SMEs. Business model innovation frameworks may serve as a valuable foundation for exploring and integrating emerging technologies, such as artificial intelligence, to support the formulation of digital business models in SMEs. In the current chapter, the business model innovation framework proposed by Ramdani *et al.* (2019) was adopted to conceptualise SMEs' digital business models that integrate emerging technologies. This framework builds on the work of Johnson, Christensen and Kagermann (2008), Zott and Amit (2010), and Osterwalder and Pigneur (2010), focusing on areas of innovation where alternative or new business models can be considered or developed, and on how to address the changes in business models over time. The business model innovation framework presents business models by incorporating key components of innovation identified by Ramdani *et al.* (2019). These components include the "why," which focuses on the value proposition and consists of the core offering, customer needs, target customers, and perceived customer value. The "what" pertains to the operational value and covers vital assets, key processes, partner networks, and distribution channels. Furthermore, the "how much" aspect considers cost structures, cash flow, margin and revenue models, while the "who" part delves into organisational learning, skills and competencies, incentives, and training.

Value Proposition (Why?)

Eyring, Johnson and Nair (2014) indicate that developing new business models typically begins with articulating a unique customer value proposition, the first aspect of innovation that addresses the "Why" questions. This value proposition focuses on understanding and solving customers' problems by offering new products or services (Motjolopane & Seaba, 2022). Furthermore, Eyring Johnson and Nair (2014) indicate that enterprises with innovative business models meet customers' needs at affordable prices and are likely to experience growth opportunities. This is because customers in these markets may need help to afford the cheapest high-end offerings. Al-Debei and Avison (2010) noted that modern organisations are highly focused on innovation in the value proposition to attract and retain a significant portion of their customer base. Wu *et al.*, (2010) advocated secondary business model innovation in latecomer firms to leverage disruptive technologies in emerging markets. They suggested tailoring the original business model to cater to price-sensitive mass customers and developing an attractive value proposition for the local market. The value proposition involves three main aspects: exploring new customer needs, re-evaluating the products or services offered by a company, and determining whether customers perceive the benefits provided by SMEs. The value proposition should address a specific customer need that is crucial for accomplishing an important task, as noted by Johnson, Christensen and Kagermann (2008). It is essential to consider the customer's perspective and recognise the significance of their situation. However, the value offered by SMEs must also have economic value for at least one of the parties involved, demonstrating the value created for the customer (Chesbrough & Rosenbloom, 2002). Additionally, SMEs must describe, analyse, manage, and communicate a company's sustainable value proposition to customers and other stakeholders (Jablonski, 2018). Schaltegger, Hansen and Lüdeke-Freund (2016) further stated that communicating value proposition entails explaining how the SME creates and delivers value, as well as how the SME captures economic value while preserving or replenishing natural, social and financial resources beyond its organisational limits.

Operational Value (What?)

Operational value addresses "What" questions regarding configuring essential assets and activities to deliver the value proposition. The "what" includes establishing connections with key partners and suppliers and using various channels to engage with customers (Ramdani *et al.*, 2019). The value configuration illustrates how value is generated for the target customer and identifies the crucial activities, resources, and partners involved (Richardson, 2008). The target customer component determines the specific audience the company aims to value and outlines the customer relationship strategies employed for each market segment (Osterwalder, 2010). Therefore, resources and actions need to be acquired and organised within the value configuration to enhance the quality of the offering, taking into account customer preferences and competitive factors (Hedman & Kalling, 2003). As highlighted by Al-Debei and Avison (2010), a business innovation model can be achieved through effective resource configuration, demonstrating the firm's capability to integrate various assets in a manner that effectively delivers its value proposition. Furthermore, Dahan *et al.* (2010) suggest joint cross-sector partnerships and collaboration to develop new business models involving multiple organisations. Such partnerships enable SMEs to access resources they would otherwise have to build or acquire independently.

Human Capital (Who?)

Human capital addresses the "Who" questions within a business model. Envisioning fresh approaches to conducting business, harnessing the skills and competencies necessary for developing new business models, and motivating and engaging individuals in the innovation process are key factors (Ramdani *et al.*, 2019). As noted by Belenzon and Schankerman (2015), the ability to access a pool of talent is closely tied to the specific business model chosen by managers, who can strategically influence the contributions of individuals and their impact on organisational performance. SMEs can also utilise incentives or rewards to motivate employees to fulfill their roles and meet customer demands (Sorescu *et al.*, 2011). Therefore, SMEs should establish incentive policies and review their incentive systems, as these factors can significantly affect organisational performance and growth (Roberge, 2015). Governance is another crucial element in business model design. Zott and Amit (2010) highlight that alternative business models can be explored through innovative governance approaches or by altering the entities responsible for carrying out various activities. Additionally, the study by Michel (2014) indicates that cross-functional teams have been successful in rapidly achieving business model innovation in workshops by devising novel ways to capture value.

Financial Value (How?)

The financial value addresses the "How" questions by focusing on various aspects, including generating revenue streams, modifying price-setting mechanisms, and evaluating a business's economic sustainability and profitability (Demil & Lecocq, 2010). Furthermore, the financial value represents the profit model for creating and delivering value to the target customer, with the cost structure representing monetary value associated with creating and delivering value (Richardson, 2008); SMEs need to consider their cost structures, which include expenses such as software and hardware, subscriptions, sales and marketing, implementation and adoption of AI technology, technical skills training, brokerage, ongoing maintenance, and human resources, to provide services to customers. Michel (2014) suggests that exploring alternative business models can involve changing the price-setting mechanism and the price carrier. Additionally, Hinterhuber and Lizoiu (2012) indicate that companies must possess advanced pricing skills as the ability to set prices effectively impacts the revenue model. Thus, SMEs may adopt a dynamic pricing model for their services, such as customer value-based pricing, cost-based pricing, or competition-based pricing. Business model innovation, therefore, involves exploring new approaches to generating cash flows.

Business Model Canvas

Osterwalder and Pigneur (2010) describe the business model canvas as a conceptual tool for developing a business model. It serves as a blueprint for implementing the business strategy, as highlighted by Duvaut *et al.* (2020). The canvas defines how values are communicated to the target audience and outlines the partnerships in marketing, supply chain, and cash flow (Osterwalder & Pigneur, 2010). Fig. **(1)** visually represents the components of the business model canvas, as outlined by Osterwalder and Pigneur (2010).

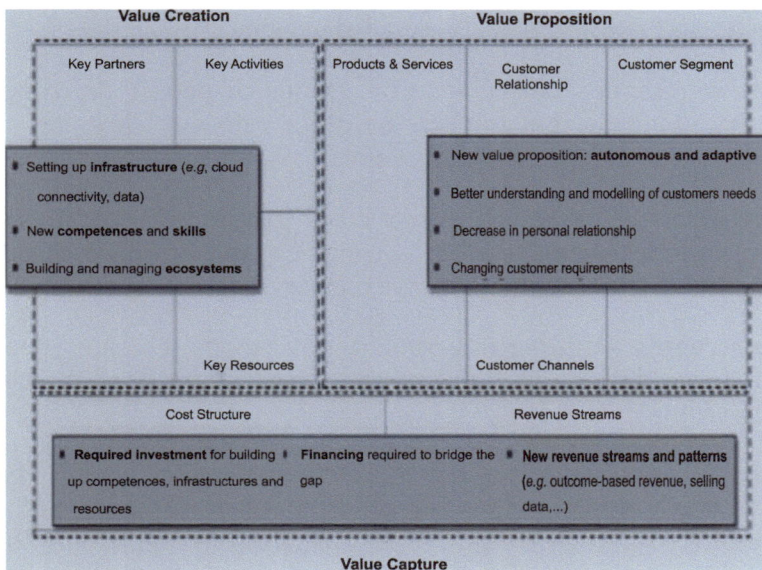

Fig. (1). Business model canvas (Osterwalder & Pigneur, 2010).

Osterwalder and Pigneur (2010) identified and described nine pathways within the business canvas model that facilitate business innovation. These pathways include:

• **Key partners** - encompass the network of suppliers and collaborators necessary for the business to operate effectively.

• **Key activities -** refer to the crucial tasks and operations that the enterprise must undertake to ensure the success of its business models, such as software development, supply chain management, or consultancy.

• **Key resources** - include the essential human, financial, or knowledge-based assets to sustain the business model's operations.

• **Value proposition** - outlines the core value of a product or service that can be communicated to customers, highlighting its unique qualities and how it differentiates from competitors.

• **Customer relationship -** details the interactions and connections the enterprise establishes with its customers and strategies for maintaining and strengthening these relationships.

• **Channels -** serve as the means through which the enterprise reaches and engages with its customers, encompassing various communication and distribution channels and facilitating the delivery of the value proposition.

• **Customer segments -** define specific groups of people the company targets based on shared needs, behaviours, or other relevant attributes, focusing on elements that generate the highest revenue.

• **Cost structure -** describes the direct costs incurred in operating the business model. Some models prioritise cost efficiency and optimisation, while others emphasise providing a premium user experience.

• **Revenue streams -** outline the primary sources of revenue generated by the business model, which can include one-time transactions or recurring, predictable income in the future.

These nine business model canvas elements, along with the element's interconnectedness, serve as the underlying business logic of the company that may be used to assist SMEs digital transformation in identifying their available resources and capabilities, enabling SMEs to align their resources and capabilities with market demands and requirements in a digital environment.

METHODOLOGY

This chapter offers insights into the digital transformation of business model innovation in SMEs. The interaction of organisations forms a business network and how they function as a unit, sustaining and transforming one another. Based on this, the Critical Realism approach was found to help describe the construct of business model innovation because it reflects its dynamic interactional nature in terms of ontology (view of the nature of reality), epistemology (theory of the nature of knowledge), and methodology (view of the appropriate ways to study knowledge). The methodology is thus founded on the basic principles of Critical Realism, namely the existence of a structured real world, the fact that learning is socially produced, and the pursuit of the generative mechanisms that help us understand empirical experiences. A Critical Realism method was employed, involving a critical examination of the relevant literature concerning the application of artificial intelligence for digital transformation in South African SMEs. The literature review followed a protocol-driven approach, ensuring selecting, analysing, and evaluation relevant articles to establish reliable and repeatable results (Vaska *et al*., 2021).

The review protocol included the following components: *Inclusion/Exclusion Criteria:* To encompass all pertinent studies, a content analysis focusing on the digital transformation in South African SMEs by adopting Artificial Intelligence was conducted. This analysis involved databases such as Google Scholar, Springer, Scopus, JSTOR, EBSCOhost, and Web of Science. Editorials, theses, books, and articles unrelated to the digital transformation of SMEs through AI adoption were excluded from the chapter. *The Search Strategy*: Specific keywords and search terms were utilised to gather data from relevant studies reporting on the digital transformation of SMEs through the adoption of artificial intelligence. The presence of these keywords in the article titles and abstracts was checked after conducting the initial search to ensure alignment with the study's research objectives. The study s selection encompassed systematic literature reviews that focused on the digital transformation of SMEs through the adoption of artificial intelligence technology. The retrieved articles underwent screening in two rounds. Overall, this process ensured a complete and rigorous examination of literature to shed light on the digital transformation of business models in SMEs using AI technologies.

The screening process for the retrieved articles consisted of two rounds. In the first round, some articles, including duplicates, were eliminated after a thorough reading, as they were found to be irrelevant to the research objectives, resulting in a reduced sample size. The second round involved an iterative screening process, identifying all relevant articles. Out of the initial 250 reports, 160 duplicates were removed, leaving 90 articles for relevance assessment based on inclusion criteria. 42 articles were deemed irrelevant and excluded, while 48 articles were evaluated for eligibility. Subsequently, 26 articles that did not align with the scope of the review were excluded. Finally, 22 articles that met the inclusion criteria, focusing primarily on the digital transformation of SMEs through the adoption of artificial intelligence technology, were included in the final review. The systematic literature review process is illustrated in Fig. **(2)**.

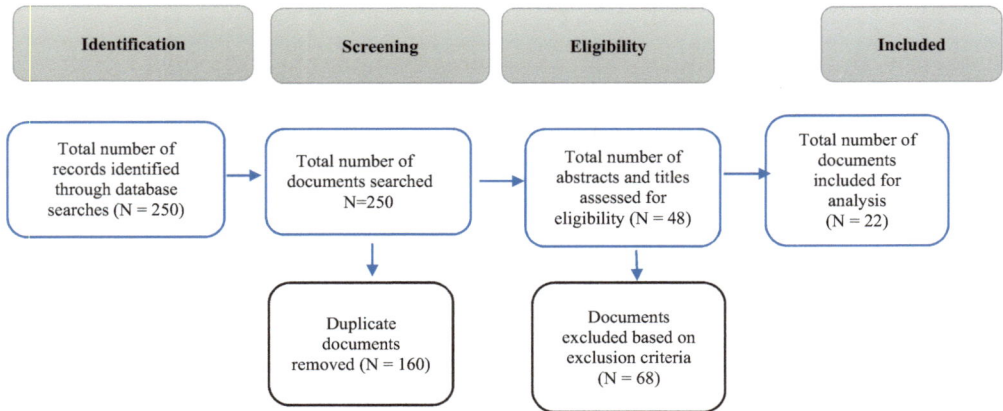

Fig. (2). Flow chart of the study selection process for the systematic review guided by the PRISMA method.

DATA ANALYSIS AND FINDINGS

The qualitative data extracted from previous studies, specifically those addressing the digital transformation of SMEs through the adoption of artificial intelligence technology, was analysed using a descriptive-analytical narrative method. The findings are organised and presented according to the following themes, aligned with the research objectives that included the impact of digital transformation on business operations and processes in SMEs, strategies for effectively developing business model innovation and Artificial intelligence as a catalyst for digital business models in SMEs. The first theme explores how digital transformation affects various aspects of business operations and processes within SMEs.

The Impact of Digital Transformation on Business Operations and Processes in Small and Medium-sized Enterprises

The digital transformation process involves the incorporation of digital technologies into the operational functions of companies, replacing physical operations with digital ones (Kohli & Melville, 2019). The widespread adoption and integration of advanced technologies such as artificial intelligence and digitally enabled infrastructures have fundamentally altered the nature of products and services across most if not all, SMEs (Marcel *et al.*, 2022). Emerging technologies such as artificial intelligence, blockchain, robotics, the Internet of Things and 3D printing have significantly changed the economy and the business landscape. Digital innovation reshapes product and service development, production, and utilisation (Nambisan *et al.*, 2017). As stated by Nambisan *et al.* (2017), digital innovation involves creating business processes and models using digital technologies. With the increasing prevalence of digital innovation, a growing range of digital artefacts offer further opportunities for digitisation and digitalisation (Gradillas & Thomas, 2021).

Parida, Sjodin, and Reim (2019) define digital transformation or digitalisation as utilising technologies to innovate the business model and create additional revenue and value-generation opportunities. Their work also offers an overview of how digitalisation can drive business model innovation in the service industry, focusing on the processes of value creation, proposition, and capture. Hakanen and Rajala (2018) emphasise that digital transformation can support successful innovations by enabling firms to create new offering configurations, enhance their understanding of customer needs, and collaborate with external actors. Digital transformation impacts various aspects of a business, including processes, practices, services, and products, and can lead to significant business model innovations. Profiting from digital advancements necessitates significant reconfigurations in activities, resources, partnerships, offerings, customer relationships, channels, and cost and revenue models (Parida *et al.*, 2019). Business model innovation plays a strategic role in acquiring and maintaining competitive advantages and determining a firm's long-term survival (Di Toma & Ghinoi, 2020). Numerous studies highlight the importance of business model innovation for firm survival, performance, and competitive advantage (Amit & Zott, 2012; Baden-Fuller & Haefliger, 2013; Casadesus-Masanell & Zhu, 2013). Visnjic, Neely and Jovanovic (2018) further explore the benefits of digitalization-led business model innovation, emphasising revenue growth and operational efficiency opportunities. Business model innovation represents an organisational innovation through which firms explore new ways to define the value proposition and create and capture value for customers, suppliers, and partners (Casadesus-Masanell & Zhu, 2013). The business model concept encompasses the firm's solutions, the activities and processes employed to deliver value, and the earning logic to cover costs and generate profits (Bouncken & Aslam, 2019). It essentially captures the business logic of a firm, focusing on value creation rather than competition (Teece & Linden, 2017). Furthermore, Motjolopane and Ruhode (2021) define a business model as the underlying economic rationale for how a business generates revenue and creates value for its target customers, considering key activities, resources, partnerships, and value exchanges between the company and its partners.

However, the emergence of new digital products and services brings significant management challenges and unprecedented opportunities for established companies and new players in the market (Nambisan *et al.*, 2017). Incumbent companies often struggle to fully leverage the opportunities presented by digital technologies due to the requirement of fundamentally different capabilities for many digital innovations. This often necessitates collaboration with partners who already possess these capabilities, leading to changes in the industry structure (Vaskelainen *et al.*, 2021). Adopting digital technologies enables new products and services and facilitates new ways of organising and the potential for disruptive business model innovations, introducing additional challenges (Sund *et al.*, 2021). Furthermore, integrating material technologies with information allows digitally enabled products to connect complexly, posing challenges in managing the innovation process (Tilson *et al.*, 2010). Developing platforms and ecosystems alongside products and services adds further complexity to the innovation process, creating management challenges and risks that managers often need help to address (Adner & Feiler, 2019).

Strategies for Effective Development of Business Model Innovation

Scholars have a growing consensus that firms must continuously change, adapt, and innovate their business models to leverage technological advancements and achieve long-term success effectively (Baden-Fuller & Haefliger, 2013). The dynamics of value creation have led to the displacement of top-performing firms from various industries, emphasising the need for firms to evolve their business models in response to the changing business environment (Jacobides & MacDuffie, 2013). Staying with outdated business models without adapting to the evolving landscape puts even successful firms at risk of failure (Doz & Kosonen, 2010). Achtenhagen, Melin, and Naldi (2013) further emphasise the importance of continuous business model changes to ensure sustained value creation and capture. Thus, calling for SMEs to adapt business models, more so in a rapidly digitising environment.

In this context, Jacobides and MacDuffie (2013) introduce the concept of value migration, which refers to the shifting of value-creating forces over time that impact firms' profitability. This perspective underscores the need for business model innovation as value migrates from outdated business designs to new ones that better address customers' needs and preferences. Value migration can occur across industries, within different business units or products, or from obsolete business models to new ones that align with customers' priorities (Slywotzky, 1996). Value migration represents the movement of economic and shareholder value away from outdated models towards those that effectively create utility for customers and generate profits for the company. While some firms may achieve value inflow due to changes in their business models, others will experience value outflow (firms lose value to other firms) because of business models that have become less competitive or even outdated (Slywotzky (1996). Value migration underscores that SMEs must develop business model innovation to remain competitive. Casadesus-Masanell and Tarzijan (2012) argue that firms may need to use distinct business models to outperform competitors, forestall potential disruptors, enter new markets, make more efficient use of resources, or develop new income streams. As outlined by Jabłonski (2018), the three stages of value migration include value inflow, whereby a company or an industry captures value from other sectors or companies due to superior value proposition. The company or industry's market share and profit margins expand at this stage. Stability, whereby competitive equilibrium is established and growth rates moderate and value outflow, whereby value starts to move away towards companies or industries meeting evolving customer needs (Duggad, 2017). However, business model innovation may be challenging while some companies may experience value inflow; others may face value outflow as business models become less competitive or outdated (Slywotzky, 1996). Value migration highlights SMEs' need for business model innovation to maintain competitiveness. Casadesus-Masanell and Tarzijan (2012) indicate that companies may adopt distinct business models to outperform competitors, pre-empt potential disruptors, enter new markets, optimise resource utilisation, or develop new revenue streams. Jabłonski (2018) identified the three stages of value migration including value inflow, where a company or industry captures value from others by offering superior value propositions, leading to expanded market share and profit margins. The stability stage is characterised by establishing competitive equilibrium and moderate growth rates. In contrast, the value outflow stage sees value moving away from firms or industries that fail to meet evolving customer needs (Duggad, 2017).

In undertaking business model innovation, SMEs can enhance their primary business model by aligning it with the external business environment (Hacklin *et al.*, 2018). This transformation of the direct business model aligns with the dynamic capability perspective, emphasising a firm's ability to adapt and change in response to the environment as a critical determinant of success over time (Achtenhagen *et al.*, 2013). Teece (2010) suggests that enterprises must continuously sense, seize, and transform to remain competitive. However, as Johnson and Suskewicz (2009) indicate, business model changes are often necessary for industries facing structural shifts. New ecosystems emerge, requiring companies to reinvent value creation and capture to stay relevant.

Business model innovation is critical in dynamic environments where value rapidly migrates between companies. Business model innovation enables companies to undergo iterative cycles of learning and experimentation to properly match firm capabilities with market needs, lowering the risk of short- and long-term strategic failure (Casadesus-Masanell & Tarzijan, 2012). In addition, pivoting the primary business model enhances product-market fit, is more likely to lead to successful value creation and capture compared to reactive changes and results in higher rates of value creation and capture compared to launching parallel secondary business models (Hacklin *et al.*, 2018). Slywotzky (1996) noted that when value starts to migrate, the firm's ability to create and capture value becomes immediately threatened, leading to resource reallocating and redeployment.

Artificial Intelligence as a Driver for Digital Business Model Innovation (DBMI) in SMEs

There is a significant shift towards digital transformation, characterised by the integration of Artificial Intelligence (AI), learning algorithms, and the Internet of Things, revolutionising work practices across small and large businesses (Leonardi & Treem, 2020). Digital transformation involves incorporating digital technologies into various business processes, offering opportunities to integrate products and services across different boundaries, be it functional, organisational, or geographic (Sebastian *et al.*, 2017). Among these transformative technologies, AI stands out as a driving force behind profound economic changes. The adoption of AI is increasing rapidly, fuelled by the desire to enhance customer experience, improve employee efficiency, and accelerate innovation, as highlighted by the International Data Corporation (2020). While there are initial deployments of AI applications, such as video suggestions, production recommendations, spam filters, and navigation systems, these are just the beginning stages (Deloitte, 2017). AI technologies are catalysts for change and have the potential to bring about substantial transformations across various industries, challenging the existing business models and norms and driving technological advancements (Bharadwaj *et al.*, 2013).

The advent of digital technologies has thus sparked a transformative wave across industries, giving rise to the concept of "Industry 4.0" or the "smart factory" (Lasi *et al.*, 2014). This digital transformation revolutionises business operations and paves the way for emerging new business practices and innovative models through emerging technologies. Demil *et al.* (2015) emphasise that business model innovation is a dynamic concept that requires continuous adaptation to meet the changing conditions of the business ecosystem. Kumar, *et al.* (2020) state that the innovation process aims to generate profits for SMEs by creating new sales opportunities, driving income growth on existing platforms, and achieving time, resource, efficiency, and performance improvements. Intelligent and innovative technologies such as machine learning, blockchain, and AI can revolutionise current processes, develop novel business models, and drive industry-wide transformations (Nguyen *et al.*, 2018). Therefore, SMEs should explore integrating these intelligent technologies to maximise their benefits across their processes and products. Adopting artificial intelligence technology is increasingly becoming a strategic choice for SMEs, enabling them to reduce operational costs, improve efficiency, drive revenue growth, and enhance the overall customer experience.

The introduction of AI has significantly impacted businesses of all sizes, with even newcomers to these technologies able to reap substantial benefits. Alhashmi, Salloum and Abdallah (2019) defined artificial intelligence and machine learning models as computational algorithms that use trained data and human-like experiences to make decisions compared to those made by experts with the same information. Khelifi *et al.* (2020) expanded on this, explaining that AI has traditionally been developed to perform intellectual tasks and carry out complex duties that humans previously carried out. It has the potential to enhance productivity and efficiency by automating routine procedures and functions, resulting in time and cost savings in the workplace. As noted by Sun and Stranieri (2021), the impact of artificial intelligence technologies extends to various domains such as work, life, business, management, healthcare, and finance, e-commerce, and web services, leading to a new digital business model. Digital business model innovation involves modifying firms' value propositions, delivery, and capture (Parida, Sjodin & Reim, 2019). SMEs are increasingly drawn to AI in their innovation processes due to factors like volatile and dynamic environments, intense global competition, rival technologies, and rapidly changing political landscapes, as highlighted by Spieth, Schneckenber, Ricart (2014); Jones, Golan, Hanna (2016) and O' Cass and Wetzels (2018).

Artificial intelligence technology in SMEs offers benefits such as improved control over internet branding, enhanced customer experience, and the ability to optimise business processes through comprehensive analysis and identification of desired outcomes (Manogaran *et al.*, 2021). By leveraging AI, SMEs can achieve greater efficiency and effectiveness in their operations while catering to their target audience's specific needs and preferences. Artificial intelligence technology in business innovation offers various advantages, including automation of routine tasks, increased productivity, faster decision-making, personalised customer experiences, data-driven insights, revenue growth, and enhanced expertise, enabling companies to save time and money, optimise operations, and make informed decisions based on cognitive technologies (Mishra & Tripathi, 2020). While artificial intelligence technologies excel at automating mundane and repetitive tasks, optimal performance enhancements are often achieved through collaboration between humans and machines (Wang *et al.*, 2022). Therefore, SMEs should perceive AI as a tool to enhance human capabilities rather than a replacement to leverage its potential fully.

Proposed Digital Business Model Innovation based on Artificial Intelligence

Bock and George (2014) asserted that small and big enterprises must change their primary business model to align with shifting digital demands. The chapter proposes an integrated digital business innovation model applicable to SMEs in South Africa, based on artificial intelligence and guided by the business model innovation framework by Ramdani, Binsaif and Boukrami (2019) and business model canvas by Osterwalder and Pigneur (2010), as well as enabling factors from the literature review. Fig. **(3)** depicts the proposed digital business model innovation framework based on Artificial Intelligence.

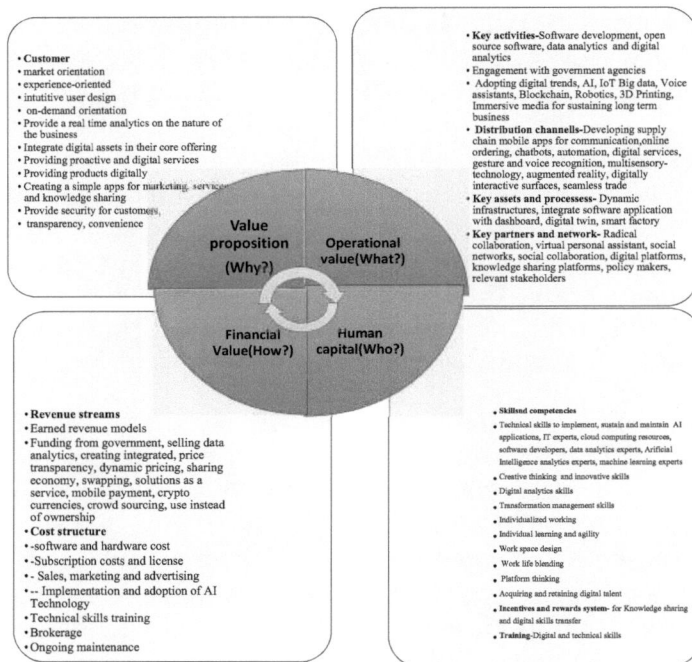

Fig. (3). Proposed Digital Business Model Innovation Framework for SMEs.

The proposed digital business model innovation framework was developed by comprehensively investigating essential needs and requirements for practical digital business innovation. It is argued that these factors play a crucial role in understanding and guiding business innovation practices, particularly in the context of sustainable digital business model innovation in SMEs in South Africa. The primary objective of this framework is to facilitate a broader comprehension of the requirements for business innovation, with a specific focus on areas where alternative business models can be explored. The study emphasises that these four interconnected circles within the framework are interdependent and cannot be separated from each other. Therefore, Their combination is central to the future and success of digital business innovation practices within South African SMEs.

CONCLUSION AND RECOMMENDATIONS

This chapter aimed to explore how SMEs may innovate business models using artificial intelligence (AI) technologies. The chapter examines the strategies and mechanisms employed by SMEs to develop, support, and enhance digital business models. While some SMEs have embraced the digital transformation era, adopting technologies such as artificial intelligence in developing and transforming their business models has been relatively slow. The successful implementation of digital transformation also requires skills in utilising digital technologies across small and large enterprises. However, incorporating artificial intelligence technologies presents challenges if employees within SMEs need more knowledge and technical skills to leverage advanced technologies for business transformation effectively. Several recommendations are proposed to facilitate the effective adoption of artificial intelligence, including implementing supportive policies, fostering collaborative partnerships, and overcoming technological obsolescence by improving technical infrastructure. SMEs should also allocate sufficient funds to embrace advanced technologies such as Artificial Intelligence, big data analytics, and the Internet of Things (IoT), to drive digital transformation operational efficiencies and business models. Furthermore, the chapter presents a framework that serves as a roadmap or guide for employees and managers seeking to enhance digital business models within SMEs. This framework highlights the crucial areas for successful business model innovation: value proposition, operational value, human capital, and financial value.

GLOSSARY

Artificial Intelligence	It is an innovative technology that has the potential to enhance business practices productivity and efficiency by automating routine procedures and functions in enterprises, resulting in time and operational cost savings, drive revenue growth, and enhance the overall customer experience. It is an innovative technology used in enhancing business practices, improving business performance, delivering brand services, and developing new business innovation strategies
Business model	It is a plan on how the business will generate revenue and reach profitability
Business model canvas	It serves as a blueprint for implementing the business strategy and developing a business model and defines how values are communicated to the target audience and also outline the partnerships in marketing, supply chain, and cash flow
Business model innovation	It is the process by which businesses create and acquire value through the organization of internal processes and external relationships with customers and suppliers. It is the value creation by making changes and supporting business' value proposition to customers and to its underlying operating model.

Digitalisation	It is the use of digital technologies to change a business models and provide new opportunities for revenue and value creation in small and large enterprises. It involves business innovation that creates new opportunities for innovating customer experiences streamlining processes, and building new business models.
Digital innovation	It involves creating business processes and models using emerging digital technologies.
Digital technologies	Refers to digital tools, devices, systems and resources utilized by enterprises in processing or storing data and performing many other business functions, such as implementing, increasing business efficiency and productivity, automating customer service, improving sales efficiency, increasing employee performance etc. The emerging disruptive technologies include artificial intelligence, the Internet of Things and big data analytics, to name a few.
Digital transformation	It is the process by which small and large enterprises are adopting implementing and integrating digital technologies in all areas of their businesses to drive fundamental change by creating new or modify existing products, services and operations as well as increasing value through innovation, invention, customer experience or efficiency.
Small and medium-sized enterprises	Refers to businesses that fall below certain revenue and most of the businesses with less than 500 employees are considered to be SMEs. However, these limits vary between countries with professional and government agencies determining the thresholds in each country or region.
Value migration	It refers to the shifting of value-creating forces over time that impact firms' profitability. It is migration of value from outmoded or outdated business models to business designs which are better able to satisfy customers or consumer's priorities.

REFERENCES

Achtenhagen, L, Melin, L & Naldi, L (2013) Dynamics of business models Strategizing, critical capabilities and activities for sustained value creation. *Long Range Plann,* 46, 427-42.
[http://dx.doi.org/10.1016/j.lrp.2013.04.002]

Adner, R & Feiler, D (2019) Interdependence, perception, and investment choices: An experimental approach to decision making in innovation ecosystems. *Organ Sci,* 30, 109-25.
[http://dx.doi.org/10.1287/orsc.2018.1242]

Akpan, IJ, Soopramanien, D & Kwak, DH (2020) Cutting-edge technologies for small business and innovation in the COVID-19 global health pandemic era. *J Small Bus Entrep,* 1-11.
[http://dx.doi.org/10.1080/08276331.2020.1799294]

Al-Debei, MM & Avison, D (2010) Developing a unified framework of the business model concept. *Eur J Inf Syst,* 19, 359-76.
[http://dx.doi.org/10.1057/ejis.2010.21]

Alhashmi, SFS, Salloum, SA & Abdallah, S (2019) Critical success factors for implementing artificial intelligence projects in dubai government united arab emirates (uae) health sector: applying the extended technology acceptance model. *In: Hassanien, A, Shaalan, K, Tolba, M (eds) Proceedings of the International Conference on Advanced Intelligent Systems and Informatics,* Springer, Cham. 1058.

Baden-Fuller, C & Haefliger, S (2013) Business models and technological innovation. *Long Range Plann,* 46, 419-26.
[http://dx.doi.org/10.1016/j.lrp.2013.08.023]

Belenzon, S & Schankerman, M (2015) Motivation and sorting of human capital in open innovation. *Strateg*

Manage J, 36, 795-820.
[http://dx.doi.org/10.1002/smj.2284]

Bharadwaj, A, El Sawy, OA, Pavlou, PA & Venkatraman, N (2013) Digital business strategy: Toward the next generation of insights. *Manage Inf Syst Q,* 37, 471-82.
[http://dx.doi.org/10.25300/MISQ/2013/37:2.3]

Birkinshaw, J & Gibson, C (2004) Building ambidexterity into an organisation. *MIT Sloan Manag Rev,* 45, 47e55.

Casadesus-Masanell, R & Spulber, DF (2005) *Trust and incentives in the agency, South Calif Interdiscip Law J,* 15, 45e104.

Casadesus-Masanell, R & Tarzijan, J (2012) When one business model is not enough. *Harvard Business Review.*

Casadesus-Masanell, R & Zhu, F (2013) Business model innovation and competitive imitation: The case of sponsor-based business models. *Strateg Manage J,* 34, 464-82.
[http://dx.doi.org/10.1002/smj.2022]

Chesbrough, H & Rosenbloom, RS (2002) The role of the business model in capturing value from innovation: evidence from Xerox Corporation's technology spin-off companies. *Ind Corp Change,* 11, 529-55.
[http://dx.doi.org/10.1093/icc/11.3.529]

Dahan, NM, Doh, JP, Oetzel, J & Yaziji, M (2010) Corporate-NGO Collaboration: Co-creating new business models for developing markets. *Long Range Plann,* 43, 326-42.
[http://dx.doi.org/10.1016/j.lrp.2009.11.003]

Deloitte (2017) *AI and your Perceptions of Artificial Intelligence from the EMEA financial services industry.* Deloitte Consulting.

Demil, B & Lecocq, X (2010) Business model evolution: In search of dynamic consistency. *Long Range Plann,* 43, 227-46.
[http://dx.doi.org/10.1016/j.lrp.2010.02.004]

Di Toma, P & Ghinoi, S (2021) Overcoming hierarchy in business model innovation: An actor-oriented approach. *Eur J Innov Manage,* 24, 1057-81.
[http://dx.doi.org/10.1108/EJIM-10-2019-0307]

Doz, YL & Kosonen, M (2010) Embedding strategic agility. *Long Range Plann,* 43, 370-82.
[http://dx.doi.org/10.1016/j.lrp.2009.07.006]

Duggan, G (2017) *Value Migration: Picking Winners in Disruptive Times.* Motilal Oswal, Mumbai, India.

El Sawy, OA & Pereira, F (2013) Digital business models: Review and synthesis. *Business Modelling in the Dynamic Digital Space,* 13-20.

Eyring, MJ, Johnson, MW & Nair, H (2014) New business models in emerging markets. *IEEE Eng Manage Rev,* 42, 19-26.
[http://dx.doi.org/10.1109/EMR.2014.6823806]

Garzella, S., Fiorentino, R., Caputo, A., & Lardo, A. (2020). Business model innovation in SMEs: the role of boundaries in the digital era. Technology Analysis & Strategic Management, 33, 31-43.
[http://dx.doi.org/10.1080/09537325.2020.1787374]

Gradillas, M & Thomas, LDW (2021) Digi-what? Disambiguating digitisation and digitalization. IESE Working Paper, Barcelona,. Spain.

Jabłoński, M (2018) Value migration to the sustainable business models of digital economy companies on the capital market. *Sustainability,* 10, 3113.
[http://dx.doi.org/10.3390/su10093113]

Jacobides, MG & MacDuffie, JP (2013) How to drive value your way. *Harvard Business Review.*

Johnson, M, Christensen, CC & Kagermann, H (2008) Reinventing your business model. *Harv Bus Rev,* 87,

52-60.

Hacklin, F, Björkdahl, J & Wallin, MW (2018) Strategies for business model innovation: How firms reel in migrating value. *Long Range Plann,* 51, 82-110.
[http://dx.doi.org/10.1016/j.lrp.2017.06.009]

Hacklin, F, Björkdahl, J & Wallin, MW (2018) Strategies for business model innovation: How firms reel in migrating value. *Long Range Plann,* 51, 82-110.
[http://dx.doi.org/10.1016/j.lrp.2017.06.009]

Haefner, N, Wincent, J, Parida, V & Gassmann, O (2021) Artificial intelligence and innovation management: A review, framework, and research agenda. *Technological Forecasting and Social Change,* 162, 120392.
[http://dx.doi.org/10.1016/j.techfore.2020.120392]

Hakanen, E & Rajala, R (2018) Material intelligence as a driver for value creation in IoT-enabled business ecosystems. *J Bus Ind Mark,* 33, 857-67.
[http://dx.doi.org/10.1108/JBIM-11-2015-0217]

Hedman, J & Kalling, T (2003) The business model concept: Theoretical underpinnings and empirical illustrations. *Eur J Inf Syst,* 12, 49-59.
[http://dx.doi.org/10.1057/palgrave.ejis.3000446]

Hinterhuber, A & Liozu, S (2012) Is it time to rethink your pricing strategy? *MIT Sloan Manag Rev,* 53, 69-78.

Hu, B, Zhang, T & Yan, S (2020) How corporate social responsibility influences business model innovation: The mediating role of organizational legitimacy. *Sustainability,* 12, 2667.
[http://dx.doi.org/10.3390/su12072667]

Jones, LD, Golan, D, Hanna, SA & Ramachandran, M (2018) Artificial intelligence, machine learning and the evolution of healthcare. *Bone Joint Res,* 7, 223-5.
[http://dx.doi.org/10.1302/2046-3758.73.BJR-2017-0147.R1] [PMID: 29922439]

Johnson, M & Suskewicz, J (2009) How to jump-start the clean-tech economy. *Harv Bus Rev,* 87

Kohli, R & Melville, N (2019) Digital innovation: A review and synthesis. *Inf Syst J,* 29

Kraft, C, Lindeque, JP & Peter, MK (2022) The digital transformation of Swiss small and medium-sized enterprises: insights from digital tool adoption. *Journal of Strategy and Management,* 15, 468-94.
[http://dx.doi.org/10.1108/JSMA-02-2021-0063]

Kumar, V, Lai, KK, Chang, YH, Bhatt, PC & Su, FP (2021) A structural analysis approach to identify technology innovation and evolution path: a case of m-payment technology ecosystem. *J Knowl Manage,* 25, 477-99.
[http://dx.doi.org/10.1108/JKM-01-2020-0080]

Lasi, H, Fettke, P, Kemper, HG, Feld, T & Hoffmann, M (2014) Industry 4.0. *Bus Inf Syst Eng,* 6, 239-42.
[http://dx.doi.org/10.1007/s12599-014-0334-4]

Leonardi, PM & Treem, JW (2020) Behavioral Visibility: A new paradigm for organization studies in the age of digitization, digitalization, and datafication. *Organ Stud,* 41, 1601-25.
[http://dx.doi.org/10.1177/0170840620970728]

Linde, L, Frishammar, J & Parida, V (2021) Revenue models for digital servitisation: a value capture framework for designing, developing, and scaling digital services. *IEEE Transactions on Engineering Management,* 70, 82-97.
[http://dx.doi.org/10.1109/TEM.2021.3053386]

Liu, DY, Chen, S-W & Chou, T-C (2011) Resource fit in digital transformation. *Manage Decis,* 49, 1728-42.
[http://dx.doi.org/10.1108/00251741111183852]

Lu, J (2020) Artificial intelligence and business innovation. *2020 International Conference on E-Commerce and Internet Technology (ECIT).* Zhangjiajie, China, 237-40.

[http://dx.doi.org/10.1109/ECIT50008.2020.00061]

Manogaran, G, Alazab, M, Shakeel, PM & Hsu, CH (2022) Blockchain assisted secure data sharing model for internet of things based smart industries. *IEEE Trans Reliab,* 71, 348-58.
[http://dx.doi.org/10.1109/TR.2020.3047833]

Marcel, L A M (2022) Digital innovation: transforming research and practice. *Creation,* 24, 4-12.
[http://dx.doi.org/10.1080/14479338.2021.2005465]

Markides, CC & Charitou, CD (2004) Competing with dual business models: A contingency approach. *Acad Manag Exec,* 18, 22e36.
[http://dx.doi.org/10.5465/ame.2004.14776164]

Markides, CC & Oyon, D (2010) What to do against disruptive business models (when and how to play two games simultaneously. *MIT Sloan Manag Rev,* 51, 25e32.

Massaro, M, Dumay, J & Guthrie, J (2016) On the shoulders of giants: Undertaking a structured literature review in accounting. *Account Audit Account J,* 29, 767-801.
[http://dx.doi.org/10.1108/AAAJ-01-2015-1939]

Michel, S (2014) Capture more value. *Harv Bus Rev,* 92, 78-85.

Mishra, S & Tripathi, A (2021) AI business model: An integrative business approach. *J Innov Entrep,* 10, 18.
[http://dx.doi.org/10.1186/s13731-021-00157-5]

Morkunas, VJ, Paschen, J & Boon, E (2019) How blockchain technologies impact your business model. *Bus Horiz,* 62, 295-306.
[http://dx.doi.org/10.1016/j.bushor.2019.01.009]

Motjolopane, I & Ruhode, E (2021) Factors driving business model innovation in sample case studies in South Africa. *Afr J Sci Technol Innov Dev,* 1-15.

Nambisan, S, Lyytinen, K, Majchrzak, A & Song, M (2017) Digital innovation management: Reinventing innovation management research in a digital world. *Manage Inf Syst Q,* 41, 223-38.
[http://dx.doi.org/10.25300/MISQ/2017/41:1.03]

Nguyen, NT, Liu, BH, Chu, SI & Weng, HZ (2019) Challenges, designs, and performances of a distributed algorithm for minimum latency of data-aggregation in multi-channel WSNs. *IEEE Trans Netw Serv Manag,* 16, 192-205.
[http://dx.doi.org/10.1109/TNSM.2018.2884445]

O'Cass, A & Wetzels, M (2018) Contemporary issues and critical challenges on innovation in services. *J Prod Innov Manage,* 35, 674-81.
[http://dx.doi.org/10.1111/jpim.12464]

Osterwalder, A & Pigneur, Y (2010) *Business Model Generation: A Handbook for Visionaries, Game Changers and Challengers.* Wiley publishers.

Parida, V, Sjodin, D & Reim, W (2019) Reviewing the literature on digitalisation, business model innovation, and sustainable industry: Past achievements and future promises. *Sustainability,* 11, 2-18.

Peter, MK, Kraft, C & Lindeque, J (2019) Strategic action fields of digital transformation: An exploration of the strategic action fields of Swiss SMEs and large enterprises. *Journal of Strategy and Management,* 13, 161-79.

Ramdani, B, Binsaif, A & Boukrami, E (2019) Business model innovation: A review and research agenda. *New England Journal of Entrepreneurship,* 22, 89-108.
[http://dx.doi.org/10.1108/NEJE-06-2019-0030]

Richardson, J (2008) *The business model: An integrative framework for strategy execution* John Wiley & Sons, Ltd. 5-6.
[http://dx.doi.org/10.1002/jsc.821]

Roberge, M (2015) The right way to use compensation: To shift strategy, change how you pay your team.

Harv Bus Rev, 70-5.

Schallmo, D, Williams, CA & Boardman, L (2017) digital transformation of business models-best practice, enablers, and roadmap. *Int J Innov Manage,* 21, 1740014.
[http://dx.doi.org/10.1142/S136391961740014X]

Schaltegger, S, Hansen, EG & Lüdeke-Freund, F (2016) Business models for sustainability. *Organ Environ,* 29, 3-10.
[http://dx.doi.org/10.1177/1086026615599806]

Schoemaker, PJH, Heaton, S & Teece, D (2018) Innovation, dynamic capabilities, and leadership. *Calif Manage Rev,* 61, 15-42.
[http://dx.doi.org/10.1177/0008125618790246]

Sebastian, IM (2017) How big old companies navigate digital transformation. *MIS Q Exec,* 16, 197-213.

Sohl, T, Vroom, G & Fitza, MA (2020) How much does the business model matter for firm performance? A variance decomposition analysis. *Acad Manag Discov,* 6, 61-80.
[http://dx.doi.org/10.5465/amd.2017.0136]

Sorescu, A, Frambach, RT, Singh, J, Rangaswamy, A & Bridges, C (2011) Innovations in retail business models. *J Retailing,* 87, S3-S16.
[http://dx.doi.org/10.1016/j.jretai.2011.04.005]

Spieth, P, Schneckenberg, D & Ricart, JE (2014) Business model innovation – state of the art and future challenges for the field. *R & D Manag,* 44, 237-47.
[http://dx.doi.org/10.1111/radm.12071]

Stich, V & Hering, N (2015) Daten und Software als entscheidender Wettbewerbsfaktor, Industrie 4.0, Zeitschrift fur Integrierte Produktionsprozesse, 8-13.

Sun, Z (2021) An Introduction to Intelligent Analytics. Intelligent Analytics with Applications.
[http://dx.doi.org/10.13140/RG.2.2.32783.71843]

Sun, Z & Stranieri, A (2021) The Nature of Intelligent Analytics. In: Sun, Z. *Intelligent Analytics with Advanced Multi-industry Applications* IGI-Global, Hershey 1-22.
[http://dx.doi.org/10.4018/978-1-7998-4963-6.ch001]

Sund, KJ, Bogers, MLAM & Sahramaa, M (2021) Managing business model exploration in incumbent firms: A case study of innovation labs in European banks. *J Bus Res,* 128, 11-9.
[http://dx.doi.org/10.1016/j.jbusres.2021.01.059]

Slywotzky, AJ (1996) *Value Migration: How to Think Several Moves Ahead of the Competition.* Harvard Business Press, Boston.

Tavoleti, E (2020) *Business model innovation and digital transformation in global management consulting firms. Business Model Innovation in Global MCFs.*

Teece, DJ (2010) Business models, business strategy and innovation. *Long Range Plann,* 43, 172-94.
[http://dx.doi.org/10.1016/j.lrp.2009.07.003]

The Organization for Economic Co-operation and Development (OECD) (2017) *Enhancing the contributions of SMEs in a global and digitalised economy* 7-8.

Tilson, D, Lyytinen, K & Sørensen, C (2010) Research Commentary—Digital Infrastructures: The Missing IS Research Agenda. *Inf Syst Res,* 21, 748-59.
[http://dx.doi.org/10.1287/isre.1100.0318]

Travaly, Y & Muvunyi, K (2020) *The future is intelligent: Harnessing the potential of artificial intelligence in Africa.*Brookings Institute, Washington, DC.

Vaska, S, Massaro, M, Bagarotto, EM & Dal Mas, F (2021) The digital transformation of business model innovation: A structured literature review. *Front Psychol,* 11, 539363.
[http://dx.doi.org/10.3389/fpsyg.2020.539363] [PMID: 33584396]

Vaskelainen, T, Münzel, K, Boon, W & Frenken, K (2022) Servitisation on consumer markets: Entry and strategy in Dutch private lease markets. *Innovation (North Syd)*, 24, 231-50.
[http://dx.doi.org/10.1080/14479338.2021.1915791]

Vils, L, Mazzieri, MR, Rodrigues, GV, Da Silva, AR & Queiroz, MJ (2017) Business model innovation: A bibliometric review. *International Journal of Innovation*, 5, 311-24.
[http://dx.doi.org/10.5585/iji.v5i3.243]

Visnjic, I, Neely, A & Jovanovic, M (2018) The path to outcome delivery: Interplay of service market strategy and open business models. *Technovation*, 72-73, 46-59.
[http://dx.doi.org/10.1016/j.technovation.2018.02.003]

Wang, Z, Li, M, Lu, J & Cheng, X (2022) Business Innovation based on artificial intelligence and Blockchain technology. *Inf Process Manage*, 59, 102759.
[http://dx.doi.org/10.1016/j.ipm.2021.102759]

Wu, X, Ma, R & Shi, Y (2010) How do latecomer firms capture value from disruptive technologies? A secondary business-model innovation perspective. *IEEE Trans Eng Manage*, 57, 51-62.
[http://dx.doi.org/10.1109/TEM.2009.2033045]

Yoo, Y, Boland, RJ, Jr, Lyytinen, K & Majchrzak, A (2012) Organizing for innovation in the digitized world. *Organ Sci*, 23, 1398-408.
[http://dx.doi.org/10.1287/orsc.1120.0771]

Yunus, M, Moingeon, B & Lehmann-Ortega, L (2010) Building social business models: Lessons from the grameen experience. *Long Range Plann*, 43, 308-25.
[http://dx.doi.org/10.1016/j.lrp.2009.12.005]

Zott, C & Amit, R (2010) Business model design: An activity system perspective. *Long Range Plann*, 43, 216-26.
[http://dx.doi.org/10.1016/j.lrp.2009.07.004]

CHAPTER 5

Understanding the Affordances of Expert Systems in Improving the Competitiveness of South African Insurance SMEs

Stevens P. Mamorobela[1,*]

[1] *Department of Informatics, Faculty of ICT, Tshwane University of Technology, Pretoria, South Africa*

Abstract: Small and Medium Enterprises in the insurance industry of South Africa are increasingly seeking new ways to improve competitiveness. Recently, technologies like expert systems are evolving to provide new knowledge to enable organizations to deliver insurance services more effectively and efficiently. However, little information is presented in the studies of business model innovation about the affordances of expert systems in improving the competitiveness of the Small and Medium Enterprises in the insurance industry. Based on the literature review of the Resource-based view model, this chapter develops a model of the affordances of expert systems to guide Small and Medium Enterprises in the insurance industry in their effort to improve competitiveness. An explanatory mixed-method research approach was followed to collect relevant data using a questionnaire and semi-structured interviews to understand the affordances of expert systems in Small and Medium Enterprises in the insurance industry. The results of the study indicate that competitiveness can be improved if the Small and Medium Enterprises manage the expert system in five areas: (i) as a valuable resource; (ii) as a rare resource; (iii) as an inimitable resource; (iv) as a unique organizational resource; and (v) as a low-cost resource. Since the concept of business model innovation is centered on resources that generate value, this study has implications for theory and practice in the field of business model innovation, particularly in the Small and Medium Enterprises operating in the insurance industry.

Keywords: Business model innovation, Competitiveness, Competencies, Expert system, Insurance, Knowledge development, Resource-based view, Small and eedium enterprises, South africa, Valuable resources.

INTRODUCTION AND BACKGROUND

The Small to Medium Enterprises (SMEs) in South Africa are privately owned businesses that are generally characterized by a lack of access to capital and

---
[*] **Corresponding author Stevens P. Mamorobela:** Department of Informatics, Faculty of ICT, Tshwane University of Technology, Pretoria, South Africa; Tel: 0123829666; E-mail: phaphadi@gmail.com

Ignitia Motjolopane, Ephias Ruhode and Pius Adewale Owolawi (Eds.)

resources (Rajagopaul, Magwentshu & Kalidas, 2020). Notwithstanding their limitations, SMEs are very flexible and adaptable to changing demands and pressures. They are regarded as strategic partners for improving the economic status of the country due to their ability to innovate and create employment. In South Africa, the contribution made by SMEs in growing the economy is considerable, with over 50 present towards employment creation opportunities and 34 present towards the Gross Domestic Product (GDP) (Ayong & Naidoo, 2019). Indeed, South Africa is experiencing socio-economic challenges as a developing country, thus, the role of SMEs in growing the economy can never be overlooked. However, the competition for business is rife and SMEs have to compete with large organizations to strive for survival.

The rivalry among SME businesses of the same industries requires continued investment in innovative ways to improve competitiveness and business sustainability. Over the years, SME businesses have adopted technologies like artificial intelligence, big data, business intelligence, the Internet of Things, social media, cloud computing, and chatbots to improve their innovativeness and to compete in the industry (Arsawan *et al*, 2020). The nature of the SME business is flexible with dynamic capabilities to adopt the latest technologies to innovate their business models. Indeed, SMEs have flexible management structures that allow them to innovate. In today's business environments, digitization has become one of the main sources of innovation. The literature of business model innovation confirms that the transformation of business models accrues a lot of benefits from increased digitization (Motjolopane, Owolawi & Ruhode, 2023). Business model innovation comprises all processes and efforts for developing and enhancing business models (Motjolopane & Ruhode, 2021). Central to business model innovation is the ability to holistically describe the business model to identify and suggest areas that can benefit from the digitized innovation.

The benefits of digitization are also realized in the insurance industry where the core of the business is to manage volumes of data about the spread of risks, lasting investments, and financial stability (Olarewaju & Msomi, 2021). Since the COVID-19 pandemic struck the world, SMEs in the insurance industry have been inundated with many expectations from customers. Understandably, customers want a fast-paced insurance service that is accurate to respond to their demands. COVID-19 has triggered many uncertainties where people had to ask a lot of questions about the accuracy of insurance services and pricing thereof (Santoso, Prabowo, Warnars & Fajar, 2021). At the heart of the insurance business is the ability to determine accurate premiums which are largely influenced by the risk categorization of the objects under the insurance cover (Rawat *et al.*, 2021). This tasks can be very complex and requires very unique and rare expertise.

The emergence of technologies like expert systems offers many opportunities to SMEs in the insurance industry to effectively and efficiently deliver insurance services (Santoso *et al.*, 2021). Expert systems work at the highest level of expertise by simulating the decision making processes of humans using the knowledge that is well-defined. For example, during the process of assessing the risk profile of the customer, the expert system can facilitate communication processes between the insurance company and the customer by using the data about the claims made by the customer overtime and the knowledge of the underwriting process. This chapter presents a model for understanding the affordances of expert systems in improving the competitiveness of SMEs in the insurance industry. The structure of the chapter includes the introduction and background, research problem, purpose and objectives, research methodology, literature of the affordances of expert systems, the development of a model of the affordances of expert systems, discussions, limitations and future research direction, and conclusion.

RESEARCH PROBLEM

The ability of expert systems to solve complex problems in the insurance business processes implies that expert systems are valuable resources for organizations in the insurance industry with the potential to improve competitiveness. Evidently, expert systems contribute to the dimensions of innovation within the research of business model innovations. The inclusion of expert systems as innovations within the business models of the insurance organizations offers a lot of potential to enhance competitiveness. Indeed, business models enable the interlinks between innovative technologies and competitiveness (Baden-Fuller & Haefliger, 2013). In concurrence, Matt, Hess & Benlian, (2015) also add that business model innovation puts emphasis on value creation through innovation, a concept which is clearly interlinked with expert systems and their ability to solve complex problems using large volumes of data.

Although business model innovation research is rapidly evolving with conceptualizations and theorizations, it is still less well understood (Foss & Saebi, 2017). There are several dimensions of business model innovation research that warrant further investigation. For instance, it is not clear what could be the drivers, facilitators and hindrances of innovation within business model innovation research. Although studies of factors influencing business model innovation success are emerging (Motjolopane, & Ruhode, 2021), there is still a lack of literature that brings about an understanding of the inter-link between innovation factors and the components of the business model that are innovated. Furthermore, research into business model innovation and artificial intelligence reveals that artificial intelligence technologies are implemented practically in business, yet not theorized enough in the literature (Reim, Astrom & Erisson, 2020), perhaps reflecting that business model innovation studies are recent. As such there is a lack of comprehensive studies that bring about an understanding of the circumstances under which business model innovation gives rise to organizational competitiveness (Foss & Saebi, 2017). Thus, this study closes a theoretical gap within business model innovation studies by proposing a model for understanding the affordances of expert systems in improving the competitiveness of SMEs in the South African insurance industry.

PURPOSE AND OBJECTIVES

The purpose of this study is to develop a model for understanding the affordances of expert systems to guide SMEs in the insurance industry with their effort to improve competitiveness. This is achieved by addressing the following specific objectives:

• To determine the affordances of expert systems that are unique to SMEs competitiveness.

• To develop a model of the affordances of expert systems for SMEs in the insurance industry.

LITERATURE REVIEW

The literature on the Resource Based View (RBV) model was explored to understand how expert systems improve the competitiveness of SMEs in the insurance industry. RBV model draws its strength from its ability to analyse organizational resources that have the potential to enhance competitiveness (Chatzoglou, Chatzoudes, Sarigiannidis & Theriou, 2018). The model focuses more on identifying resources and capabilities at the disposal of an organization that has inspirational performance that is different from other competing organizations. Barney & Hesterly (2010) add that RBV assumes that a resource is valuable to enhance competitiveness if it is rare, inimitable, and cannot be duplicated nor substituted by competing firms. This holds true with how expert systems are used in the insurance industry to provide a more accurate analysis of risk factors. O'Brien Marakas (2008) laments that expert systems are cost-effective solutions that are easily adaptable. Perhaps this is one of the reasons for the growing use of expert systems in SMEs in the insurance industry.

Expert systems are information systems that use well-defined procedures for consistently executing tasks and predicting patterns of future behavior (Santoso *et al.*, 2021). The primary components making up the expert system include, the knowledge database that stores rules and heuristics about the problem domain; the inference engine which obtains knowledge from the knowledge database to make inferences based on evidence and reasoning; and the user interface which is used for communication with users of the expert system (Santoso, 2021). Expert systems are a subset of artificial intelligence technologies capable of simulating the thinking patterns of humans. Artificial intelligence can be referred to as simply the intelligence of machines resulting from the process of imitating the cognitive behavioral functions of humans (Eckert & Osterrieder, 2020). Many artificial intelligence technologies have been studied in academic literature since 1950s, with different waves of criticism, until their recent emergence in the Fourth Industrial Revolution (4IR) era (Manesh, Pellegrini, Marzi & Dabic, 2020; Liao, Deschamps, Loures & Ramos, 2017). 4IR is an era where different technological devices like the Internet of Things (IoT), artificial intelligence, nanotechnologies, robotics, cyber-physical systems, and big data are interconnected to automate most of human daily activities (Bag, Pretorius, Gupta & Dwivedi, 2021; Demlehner, Schoemer & Laumer, 2021; Hu, Lu, Pan, Gong & Yang, 2021). The demand for a world of interconnected technologies was driven by the call for organizations to become smarter in improving their innovativeness.

Research indicates that the use of artificial intelligence in organizations has the potential to increase productivity and assist with quicker decision-making processes (Dwivedi *et al.*, 2021). Gardner (2017) reports that over 59 percent of industries are growing with the use of artificial intelligence to solve complex problems and to improve decision-making. Eling & Lehmann (2018) assert that the increased efficiency and effectiveness of the insurance business relies on the ability to integrate artificial intelligence algorithms with existing processes. Indeed, artificial intelligence technologies have the potential to overhaul business. In the insurance industry, the potential for artificial intelligence technologies like chatbots, recommendation systems, knowledge-based systems, and expert systems has been explored in many areas of the business. For instance, chatbots have been studied to improve sales and marketing (Nuruzzaman & Hussain, 2020), and recommendation systems have been studied to assist insurance agents with sales projections and increased profits (Lesage, Deaconu, Lejay, Meira, Nichil & State, 2020), knowledge-based systems have been studied for their potential to improve risk analysis procedures (Joram, Harrison & Joseph, 2017).

In areas like asset management, risk management, fraud detection, and portfolio management, artificial intelligence technologies like expert systems are used to overcome the uncertainties through the management of archives and large amounts of data records (Jarrahi, 2019). Expert systems have also been studied in the insurance industry for their potential to perform evaluations of contractors (Marsh & Fayek, 2010) and automation of risk assessments for approval of loans (Sachan, Yang, Xu, Benavides & Li, 2020). Moreover, expert systems are reported to have the ability to provide a more accurate analysis of risk factors than traditional pricing methods using pattern recognition features in the sales process for insurance products (Burri, Burri, Bojja & Buruga, 2019). Because insurance involves financial transactions, expert systems can also be used to predict and avoid fraudulent claims (Eling & Lehmann, 2018). Evidently, expert systems have the potential to solve complex organizational problems facing the insurance industry (Eckert & Osterrieder, 2020). Consequently, it is becoming very essential for studies in business model innovation to investigate the affordances of expert systems in improving competitiveness. The SME environment can be very complex due to various characteristics that are used to define the context (Mamorobela, 2021; Mamorobela & Buckley, 2018). Thus, this study applies the explanatory sequential mixed methods design to develop a model for understanding the affordances of expert systems in improving the competitiveness of SMEs in the insurance industry.

CONCEPTUAL MODEL

The model for understanding the affordances of expert systems in improving the competitiveness of SMEs was conceptualised by taking into account the knowledge development and utilisation processes of the SMEs, the distinctive characteristics expert system and the SME competencies as shown in Fig. (1).

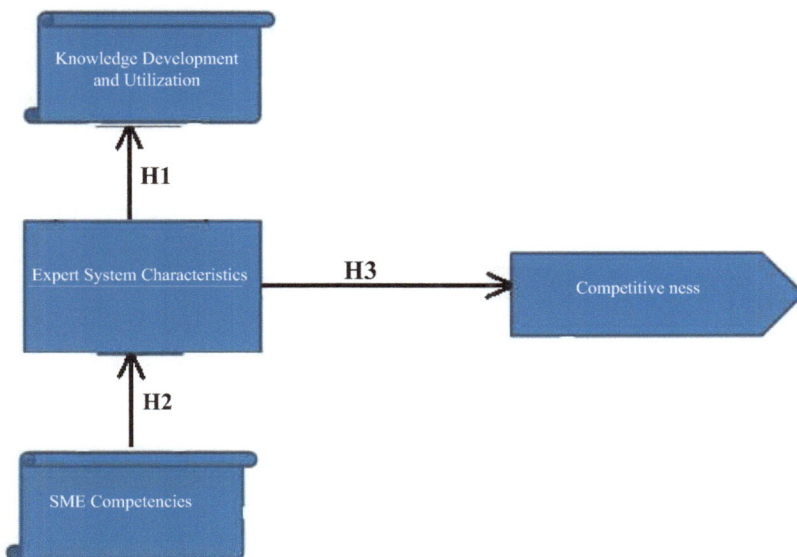

Fig. (1). Conceptual model for expert system towards improving competitiveness of SMEs. Source: Own elaboration.

Knowledge Development and Utilisation

The knowledge development and utilisation component of the model were identified to ensure that a team of experts with knowledge and skills of the insurance industry is allocated the responsibility of uplifting the expert system's knowledge database. The knowledge database must be kept recent and relevant to the specific tasks to be performed by the expert system (Mamorobela, 2016). Dima, Gabrara, Modrak, Piotr & Popescu (2010) assert that the expert systems improve organizational competitiveness through the use of accumulated knowledge and expertise. In line with this assertion, hypothesis 1 was derived as follows:

H1: Expert system positively influences the development and use of knowledge within the SME

SME Competencies

For organizations to be competent, they need to improve their ability to learn and grow. SMEs need to constantly improve their competencies by learning new ways of doing things and adopting innovative technologies to speed up their business processes (Mamorobela, 2016). Chatzoglou *et al.* (2018) assert that organizations cannot rely only on the resources to be competitive, but they need to exploit their distinctive competencies which allow them to use the resources better. As such, SME competencies become the force behind the successful implementation of expert systems resulting in superior performance and competitiveness. In concurrence, Jerab, Alper & Baslar, (2011) add that competencies and organizations are directly proportional to competitiveness. Thus, the dynamic competencies of SMEs may serve as sources of transforming the expert system into a rent-yielding core competence. This assertion was hypothesised as follows:

H2: SME competencies positively influence the performance of the expert system

Expert System Characteristics

Although the expert system provides SMEs in the insurance industry with ability to automate the risk assessment process for accurate reporting and evaluation of customers (Joram *et al.*, 2017), the characteristics for enabling such competence need to be defined in line with the expected outcomes of the SMEs (Mamorobela, 2016). This assertion was hypothesised as follows:

H3: Expert system characteristics positively influence the competitiveness of SMEs

RESEARCH METHODOLOGY

Research is a method of enquiry that follows a set of guiding principles involving different views and beliefs of the researchers in the process of understanding reality (Leedy & Ormrod, 2015). Indeed, the nature and conduct of any type of research are largely influenced by the beliefs and views of the researchers (Creswell & Creswell, 2017). Such beliefs and views formulate the philosophical assumptions that researchers make about the nature of reality. Philosophical choices like interpretivism, pluralism, positivism, and pragmatism are available for researchers to make an appropriate selection of methods to use for data collection, needed to understand reality (Ngulube 2022). Positivism and interpretivism are the dominant philosophical assumptions applied in social science research and the combination of which results in a pragmatism philosophy (Creswell & Plano-Clark, 2018).

This chapter followed a pragmatism research philosophy to select the methods that are suitable and appropriate for the research. The goal of pragmatism is centered on understanding the reality of a phenomenon using a mix of diverse approaches and methods (Ngulube, 2022). The pragmatism philosophy aims to describe a phenomenon using different perspectives and views. The different realities of research subjects are brought together in a single study to produce a comprehensive understanding of the phenomenon. This is true with the current study where the researcher adopted methods that provide understanding of the experiences of SME owners in the insurance industry with the use of expert systems and the effect of such systems on the competitiveness of their respective SMEs. The endeavor to understanding the experiences of SME owners regarding the use of expert systems, and the effect of expert systems on the competitiveness of the SMEs proved to be a very complex exercise, considering that SMEs have very dynamic business models that are not easy to comprehend (Mamorobela, 2021; Mamorobela & Buckley 2018). As such, combining both positivism and interpretivism realities (pragmatism) to construct a common understanding of the affordances of expert systems in improving the competitiveness of SMEs was a suitable research philosophy to be applied in this study.

The pragmatism philosophy afforded the study the ability to present information from different points of view to produce a holistic understanding of the affordances of expert systems in improving the competitiveness of SMEs in the insurance industry in South Africa. Although pragmatism requires a combining intepretivism and positivism in a single study (Mamorobela, 2022; Ngulube, 2022), both intepretivism and positivism philosophies can either be applied sequentially with the outcome one influencing the other, or converged and applied in parallel and the results integrated at the end. This study applied pragmatism in a sequential manner with the positivism philosophy, underpinning the quantitative approach, applied in the first phase to influence the interpretivism philosophy, underpinning the qualitative approach in the second phase of the study. This research approach strategy is referred to as the "explanatory sequential mixed methods design" (Teddlie, Johnson & Tashakkori, 2021). The explanatory sequential mixed method design is a two-part research design in which the quantitative and qualitative studies are conducted in a sequential manner (Bryman & Bell, 2015). The quantitative study is conducted first, then the qualitative follows thereafter. This is done such that the outcome of the quantitative study can influence the results of the qualitative study, meaning that the qualitative study is there to explain the findings of the quantitative study in more depth (Creswell & Creswell, 2017).

Research Setting

Access to the suitable SME owners who participated in the study was obtained through The Innovation Hub, an SME incubator organization mandated by the National Department of Small Business Development (NDSBD) to uplift the competitiveness, innovation, and entrepreneurship of SMEs in South Africa (Theinnovationhub, 2019). The researcher approached the facilities manager at The Innovation Hub, seeking a letter of approval for permission to access the profiles of SMEs on their database of 450 SMEs and to facilitate communication with the selected SME owners who met the sampling inclusion criteria. Only SMEs operating in the insurance industry were considered.

Quantitative Phase

In the first phase of the explanatory sequential mixed methods study, (the quantitative phase) the literature of the RBV was explored to derive variables that are associated with achieving competitiveness within the SME environment. The variables were then measured against the data that was collected through online questionnaires. Ngulube (2022) asserts that the explanatory sequential mixed method design has the benefit of using theoretical models in the quantitative enquiry to conceptualize the study. In concurrence, Ravitch & Riggan, (2016) add that studies that are founded in theoretical models are more rigorous and use concrete methods for gathering relevant data needed to understand the enquiry. The online questionnaire was designed to allow the participants to complete at their convenient time and location. The questionnaire was published and shared with the facilities manager at the Innovation Hub to further distribute the link to a random sample of SME owners who met the inclusion criteria to participate in the online survey. The questionnaire data were checked for normality using the central limit theorem to ensure that no missing data or outliers existed (Levine,

Szabat & Stephan, 2016). A total of 227 questionnaires were deemed usable because all questions and sections were completed, therefore the researcher closed the survey. As a result, the survey received a 50.4% response rate which was satisfactory for carrying out the structural equation modeling analysis before the data was prepared for the qualitative study in the second phase of the explanatory sequential mixed method approach (Simmon, 2011). The structural equation modeling technique was applied to produce the initial model of affordances of expert systems to be explained in more depth in the subsequent qualitative enquiry in the second phase of the study.

Qualitative Phase

In the second phase of the explanatory sequential mixed method approach, a qualitative study was carried out using semi-structured interviews with 13 SME owners who were purposively selected as respondents. The qualitative enquiry was conducted to explain the findings of the quantitative enquiry. Owing to the specific SME characteristics that are of interest to the researcher, the maximum variance purposive sampling technique was applied to select the SME owners who are knowledgeable about expert systems technologies and their application in the insurance industry. While several other purposive sampling techniques are available to researchers, it is important to note that each purposive sampling technique serves a different purpose to research studies (Creswell, 2017). For example, homogeneous purposive sampling is mainly used when the researcher wants to understand the behaviour of small groups of respondents with similar characteristics; the typical case purposive sampling technique is applied when the researcher wants to create a common understanding among samples to achieve consensus; and the extreme case purposive sampling technique aims to understand extremely unusual occurrences of the phenomenon from the selected samples. The maximum variance purposive sampling technique selects samples with an in-depth understanding of the phenomenon to share their experience from their own perspectives of the phenomenon. As such, the maximum variance purposive sampling technique was more suitable in this study to understand how expert systems could improve the competitiveness of SMEs from the perspectives of SME owners themselves.

The inclusion criteria for the maximum variance purposive sampling technique involved selecting the respondents who are the owners, founders, and directors of SMEs that are operating in the insurance industry and their SMEs have been in operation for one year and over, with the existing profile of customers. The semi-structured interviews were conducted during the time that the country was on strict lockdown due to the COVID-19 pandemic. Consequently, the researcher used online platforms like MsTeams (Microsoft 2019) to conduct the interviews.

Each interview was scheduled for 45 minutes and the researcher ensured that the time did not run over by keeping the relevant questions pertaining the use of expert systems in the insurance processes of SMEs. One major benefit derived from using MsTeams was that the platforms come with the recording and transcription features embedded in each interview. These features allowed the researcher to save the time needed in the subsequent data analysis process.

Data analysis process involved bringing order, structure and meaning to the collected interview data. In qualitative studies, it is important to ensure that the study is trust worthy (Guba & Lincoln, 1994). Trustworthiness of qualitative studies is measured by ensuring that the study is credible, meaning that the study considers the theories, models or triangulation of data (Noble & Smith, 2015); the study is dependable, meaning that the design of the study is stable such that it can be repeated by other researchers to yield similar results; the study is confirmable, meaning that the results of the study are not biased and are reported from the viewpoints of the research respondents; and that the study is transferable, meaning that the results of the study can be applied in other similar research settings. This study satisfies all the trustworthy requirements. For instance, credibility is achieved by triangulating the interview data with the literature of the RBV model; dependability is achieved by following the research onion suggested by Saunders, Lewis & Thornhill (2009) to provide a link between all aspects of the research design and the methodology; confirmability was achieved by using the codebook and the thematical analysis process to record all the relevant codes and themes derived from the interview transcripts to present the findings from the points of view of the SME owners themselves; and transferability was achieved by selecting SME owners based on their characteristics using the maximum variance purposive sampling technique which can also be used to select the respondents of similar characteristics in other research settings.

Thematical analysis was applied following the guidelines suggested by Archer *et al*. (2017). The thematic analysis procedure comprises five phases; Phase 1, text familiarization – where the researcher reads through the transcribed interviews to make sense of them and to understand how the research objectives are addressed. Phase 2, coding of the data – where the assumptions, insights, and complex motivations of the respondents are captured directly from the interview transcripts to a codebook. Phase 3, revision of the codes – where the codebook is revised to ensure that all codes are still relevant to address the objective of the study. Phase 4, theme creation – where the primary themes are created by grouping similar codes in the codebook addressing the same objective of the study; and Phase 5, revision of themes – where the themes are refined by combining related themes addressing the same research objective and discarding those which are irrelevant. The results of the qualitative enquiry of the explanatory sequential mixed method study are the final model of affordances of expert systems in improving the competitiveness of SMEs in the insurance industry. This was important to bring the understanding of such affordances to start the research debate in the area of business model innovation.

FINDINGS AND DISCUSSION

The explanatory mixed methods approach followed to validate the theoretical lenses derived from the Resource Based View (RBV) model to understand the affordances of expert systems in improving the competitiveness of SMEs in the insurance industry. Indeed, studies that are founded in theory often produce results that are unexpected, which may require validation and more explanations to produce a holistic understanding of the phenomenon (Creswell & Plano-Clark, 2018). Thus, it was appropriate to validate the variables derived from the RBV model against the data collected quantitatively using questionnaires and qualitatively through interviews to produce an understanding of the affordances of expert systems in improving the competitiveness of SMEs in the insurance industry.

FINDINGS OF THE QUANTITATIVE PHASE

The structural equation modelling technique was applied to test and confirm the validity of the proposed model of understanding the affordances of expert systems in improving the competitiveness of SMEs. Byrne (2016) laments that SEM is a confirmatory statistical technique that uses hypothesis testing to the structural models. Confirmatory factor analysis (CFA) is embedded within the SEM to assess whether the structural model is a perfect fit of the collected data. This approach was more appropriate in the current study to produce an initial model of understanding the affordances of expert systems towards improving the competitiveness of SMEs. To achieve model fitness, Hair *et al.* (2019) suggest that the results of CFA should indicate the CFI > 0.9 and RMSEA < 0.08. CFA results of this study are shown in Fig. (**2**) below:

The model fitness indexes for CFA were achieved at CFI > 0.9 and SRMR < 0.08. This indicates an acceptable fit of the model to the data (Hair *et al.*, 2019). The constructs of the proposed model were also tested for validity by means of construct validity. Pallant (2016) asserts that the constructs of the proposed model need to be accurate and relevant to ensure the quality of the data. Three types of construct validity, namely, convergent, discriminant, and nomological validity were applied. Construct validity was achieved at construct reliability (CR) > Average Variance Extracted (AVE), convergence validity was achieved at AVE > 0.5 on all constructs, discriminant validity was achieved at maximum shared variance (MSV) < AVE, and nomological validity was achieved because the observed CFA model reflected the initial relationships between constructs in the measurement model.

Measure	Estimate	Threshold	Interpretation
CMIN	1146.490	-	-
DF	427.000	-	-
CMIN/DF	2.685	Between 1 and 3	Excellent
CFI	.923	> .95	Acceptable
SRMR	.097	<.08	Acceptable
RMSEA	.086	<.08	Acceptable

Fig. (2). CFA results for model fitness indexes.

The multiple regression weights of the SEM were also tested to assess the significance of the paths for the hypothesis testing. The significance is measured using p-value ≤ 0.05 for each path (Hair *et al.*, 2019). Meaning that there is a 95% level of confidence that the path is significant. The results of the multiple regression weights and corresponding probabilities are shown in Fig. (**3**) below:

Hypothesis	Construct	Path	Construct	Un standardized Path coefficients	Standard Error of Regression Weight	Probability	Hypothesis Result
H1	KQ	<---	SysQ	-.051	.025	.040	Reject null hypothesis at α = .05
H2	SysQ	<---	SmeComp	.969	.092	P < .001	Reject null hypothesis at α = .05
H3	Compa	<---	SysQ	.411	.062	P < .001	Reject null hypothesis at α = .05

Fig. (3). Unstandardised regression weights and corresponding probabilities.

The results of the multiple regression weight indicate that the three paths for testing the hypothesis (H1, H2 and H3) were significant at p-value < 0.05. This means that the three hypotheses were supported indicating the knowledge development and utilization, SME competencies, and expert systems characteristics that are important determinants of understanding the affordances of expert systems in improving the competitiveness of SMEs.

FINDINGS OF THE QUALITATIVE PHASE

In the follow up qualitative phase of the explanatory sequential mixed methods approach followed in this study, the thematical analysis procedure was applied to explain the findings of the quantitative phase in more depth. The thematical analysis process of this study followed the guidelines of Archer, Herman, van Vuuren & Hugo (2017), suggesting the five key steps for qualitative thematical data analysis such as text familiarisation, coding of data, revision of the codes, creation of themes, and revision of the final themes. The analysis resulted in three themes being addressed and synthesised with the research questions and outcomes of the quantitative study in phase one.

Theme 1: Effect of expert system on knowledge development and utilisation in the SME

The literature of expert systems adoption was explored to guide the study with specific questions pertaining the effects of expert systems on knowledge development and use in the insurance SMEs. The interview respondents indicated that the expert system is mainly used for premium calculations and risk assessment. These findings are in line with the study of Sachan *et al.* (2020). It was interesting to discover that, although the quantitative study in phase one indicated a strong relationship between the expert system and knowledge development, the expert system does not necessarily result in knowledge generation and utilisation largely because the expert system was not formally adopted as a source for knowledge development and use in the SMEs. These sentiments were lamented by one of the respondents referring to the expert system as a blackbox system as follows:

'We probably need a team of experts to assist with constructing the blackbox system to be able to collect the information about existing processes used in each division. In my view, I think the different divisions have so much information that can be used across the board to formalise the businesses processes in a form of an automated system. Another important aspect is training of staff. Not everyone understands how to interact with the blackbox system in the company and that leads to the system not being used to its full potential.' [respondent 12]

Theme 2: SME competencies needed to support the use the expert system

It was necessary to ascertain the key SME competencies needed to support the use of the expert system in the insurance SME. This is on the back of the results of the quantitative phase which indicated that there is a strong relationship between SME competencies and the use of expert systems. The qualitative interviews also revealed that SMEs have the competencies necessary to transform the expert system into a profitable resource. Some interview respondents hinted that SMEs have some knowledge of information systems and need to include innovative technologies in the strategic agenda. For instance, one respondent expressed the position about placing information systems issues as part of organisational strategy as follows:

'The key competency is to place information systems issues at the center of its strategic mission and vision. We as SME owners and managers should support and champion technological innovations. I should also mention the ability to predict the economic value from innovative technologies like expert systems more accurately and better than the competition. However, it is still early days for us. We are still navigating around the use of technology to compete.' [respondent 3]

Theme 3: Characteristics of expert systems affecting the competitiveness of SMEs

The study of RBV theory (Chatzoglou *et al.*, 2018) suggests that that characteristics of the expert system like, value, rarity, inimitability, organisation, and cost positively affect the competitiveness of SMEs. The quantitative phase of the study also indicated that the expert system positively influences the competitiveness of the insurance SME. Given the specific characteristics of the expert system from the RBV literature, the follow-up qualitative interviews were conducted to ascertain the perception of SME owners on the effect of these characteristics on SME competence. It was discovered that SMEs derive more value from the expert systems' ability to manipulate the information for calculation of insurance premium and risk assessments. Owing to the dynamic nature of the SME business, it is much easier to exploit the expert system in all operational and strategic levels of the organization. The low-cost characteristic of the expert system is more suitable for the SME business where there are financial constraints. One of the respondents expressed their views on the characteristics of the expert system as follows:

'These expertise are unique to the SME owing the system in the insurance industry and can be very costly to develop by the competing organizations. They are developed overtime within the SME, making it almost impossible for competing organizations to imitate. Moreover, our business environment is very flexible and adaptable to adopt innovations like expert systems. We are financially constrained as SMEs and having such low cost systems means that we are able to continue with productivity at minimal costs.' [respondent 4]

LIMITATIONS AND FUTURE RESEARCH DIRECTION

This chapter contributes to the research in business model innovation by applying the explanatory sequential mixed methods approach to propose a model for understanding the affordances of expert systems in improving the competitiveness of SMEs in the insurance industry, a research area that is very complex and not well understood in the literature of business model innovations. The study applied the quantitative approach in the first phase using an online survey questionnaire to collect data across SME owners who provided some insights into the affordances of expert systems in line with the expert systems characteristics. The study was founded on the literature of the RBV where characteristics of the expert systems like value, rarity, inimitability, and organization were expounded. The literature further highlighted the aspect of cost as one other viable to be considered when trying to understand the affordance of expert systems. Understandably, cost considerations are of outmost importance for SMEs due to the financial constraints of the SME business. These characteristics were explained in-depth in the second phase of the study using the semi-structured interviews in the qualitative approach to provide more understanding of the identified affordances.

The application of the explanatory sequential mixed methods approach offered the study with the benefits of obtaining both the subjective and objective realities to understand the affordances of expert systems in improving the competitiveness of SMEs in the insurance industry. Although such benefits were derived in the study, the study was limited to a research setting which could potentially affect generalizability of results. All SME owners who participated in the study are based in The InnovationHub. However, despite the geographical location of the samples SMEs, one could argue that generalizability could be achieved if the results were to be applied in SMEs with similar characteristics, located in different parts of the country. Another limitation of the study was the number of sampled respondents in the qualitative phase of the study which could be considered to be quite small for a mixed method study (n = 13). Although qualitative studies are not mindful of the sample size (Onwuegbuzie & Collins, 2007), conducting a similar study on larger samples may unearth even more affordances than what was already discovered in this study. Nevertheless, the researcher believes that the model proposed in this study lays a good foundation for future business model innovation research discussion around the use of expert systems and their potential to improve competitiveness.

The proposed model in this study suggests that more research is needed to understand how SMEs in the insurance industry can exploit the potential of expert systems in their risk assessment processes. While the literature of business model innovation is evolving, the model proposed in this study can serve as a good contribution in this area. SMEs have very flexible organizational structures and are adaptable to changing environments. Certainly the rivalry forces within the insurance industry are vastly demanding for business agility and adaptability to remain competitive. Research efforts for understanding such fast paced and complex environments require the application of diverse methods of enquiry, and the mixed methods approach is the most suitable. The application of the explanatory sequential mixed methods approach was highly useful in this study to the determine the affordances of expert systems that are unique to SMEs competitiveness and to develop a model of the affordances of expert systems for SMEs in the insurance industry. This makes a considerable contribution to the literature of business model innovation where the aspect of innovation is given much attention. Thus, the model proposed in the study provides aspects that are deemed critical for enhancing the competitiveness of the SMEs. SMEs need to evolve through acquiring new knowledge and use technological solutions like expert systems to improve their competitiveness.

CONCLUSION

SME organizations are very dynamic and apply a variety of tools and techniques to advance their competitiveness. With expert systems evolving as one of the tools used for automating the risk management activities of the insurance industry, SMEs are starting to realize their potential and affordances. The literature on business model innovation stresses on the aspect of innovation as the driving force behind competitiveness, and the application of expected systems innovations in advancing business models is the research area that is still in its infancy. Evidently, the research that tries to understand the dynamic characteristics of SMEs is very limited. This chapter makes a significant contribution to the literature on business model innovation by proposing a model that can be used by SMEs in the insurance industry to understand the affordances of expert systems. Because the SME environment is very complex, the chapter also contributes methodologically by using the explanatory sequential mixed methods approach to produce a model for understanding the affordances of expert systems holistically. The explanatory sequential mixed methods approach was very important to produce a model based on the results of the quantitative study in the first phase which were explained further in the qualitative study, in phase two, to bring out a holistic understanding of the phenomenon. The chapter has a very important implication for SME businesses to enhance their dynamic capabilities in the business models to further their competitiveness. In particular, the chapter provides a holistic understanding of the affordances of expert systems in facilitating efforts to improve competitiveness. This area of research is not well understood and has implications for business model innovation research to delve into the practical application of expert systems in the SME environment. The explanatory sequential mixed method approach was useful in uncovering these characteristics by triangulating different sources, namely, the literature of the RBV model, the quantitative enquiry usina g survey questionnaire, and the qualitative enquiry using face-to-face semi-structured interviews. Evidently, the affordances of expert systems in improving the competitiveness of SMEs are well understood holistically using the mixed methods research approach.

GLOSSARY

Expert system	An intelligent systems that works at the highest level of expertise by simulating the decision making processes of humans using the knowledge that is well-defined.
Resource-based view model	The research model that identifies resources and capabilities at the disposal of an organization and that have inspirational performance that is different to other competing organizations
Competitiveness	The ability of an organisation to deliver better value to customers than competitors.
Business Model Innovation	The concept of value creation through innovation by making changes to the organisation's value proposition to customers and operating models.
Small and Medium Enterprises	Privately owned businesses that are generally characterized by lack of access to capital and resources.
South Africa	A country on the southernmost tip of the African continent, marked by several distinct ecosystems.
Insurance	An arrangement by which an organisation undertakes to provide a guarantee of compensation for specified loss or damage in return for payment of a specified premium
Knowledge development and utilisation	The process of acquiring, creating, storing, and distributing knowledge.
SME Competencies	The capabilities of SME to perform and compete optimally.
Valuable resources	Resources that are of great worth to the organisation and have inspirational performance that is different to other competing organizations.

REFERENCES

Archer, E, Herman, H, van Vuuren, J & Hugo, D (2017) *Introduction to Atlas ti: Basic operations, tips and tricks for coding* Research Rescue, Pretoria.

Arsawan, IWE, Koval, V, Rajiani, I, Rustiarini, NW, Supartha, WG & Suryantini, NPS (2022) Leveraging knowledge sharing and innovation culture into SMEs sustainable competitive advantage. *Int J Prod Perform Manag,* 71, 405-28.
[http://dx.doi.org/10.1108/IJPPM-04-2020-0192]

Ayong, K & Naidoo, R (2019) Modeling the adoption of cloud computing to assess South African SMEs: An integrated perspective. *In ICICIS,* 43-56.

Baden-Fuller, C & Haefliger, S (2013) Business models and technological innovation. *Long Range Plann,* 46, 419-26.
[http://dx.doi.org/10.1016/j.lrp.2013.08.023]

Bag, S, Pretorius, JHC, Gupta, S & Dwivedi, YK (2021) Role of institutional pressures and resources in the adoption of big data analytics powered artificial intelligence, sustainable manufacturing practices and circular economy capabilities. *Technol Forecast Soc Change,* 163, 120420.
[http://dx.doi.org/10.1016/j.techfore.2020.120420]

Barney, JB & Hesterly, WS (2010) VRIO Framework. In: Strategic Management and Competitive Advantage (page 68 to 86). New Jersey: Pearson.

Bryman, A & Bell, E (2015) *Business research methods* Oxford University Press.

Burri, RD, Burri, R, Bojja, RR & Buruga, SR (2019) Insurance claim analysis using machine learning algorithms. *International Journal of Innovative Technology and Exploring Engineering (IJITEE)*, 8, 577-82.

Byrne, BM (2016) *Structural equation modelling with AMOS: basic concepts, applications, and programming* Taylor & Francis Group, London.
[http://dx.doi.org/10.4324/9781315757421]

Chatzoglou, P, Chatzoudes, D, Sarigiannidis, L & Theriou, G (2018) The role of firm-specific factors in the strategy-performance relationship. *Manag Res Rev*, 41, 46-73.
[http://dx.doi.org/10.1108/MRR-10-2016-0243]

Chesbrough, H (2010) Business model innovation: Opportunities and barriers. *Long Range Plann*, 43, 354-63.
[http://dx.doi.org/10.1016/j.lrp.2009.07.010]

Creswell, JW & Creswell, JD (2017) *Research design: Qualitative, quantitative, and mixed methods approaches.* 5th ed. Sage publications, Califonia.

Creswell, JW & Plano-Clark, VL (2018) *Designing and conducting mixed methods research,* SAGE, Los Angeles.

Creswell, JW (2017) Mapping the developing landscape of mixed methods research contributors. *SAGE Handbook of Mixed Methods in Social & Behavioral Research.* 2nd ed Sage publications.

Demlehner, Q, Schoemer, D & Laumer, S (2021) How can artificial intelligence enhance car manufacturing? A Delphi study-based identification and assessment of general use cases. *Int J Inf Manage*, 58, 102317.
[http://dx.doi.org/10.1016/j.ijinfomgt.2021.102317]

Dima, IC, Gabrara, J, Modrak, V, Piotr, P & Popescu, C (2010) Using the expert systems in the operational management of production. *11th WSEAS International Conference on Mathematics and Computers in Business and Economics (MCBE'10)-Published by WSEAS Press.*

Dwivedi, YK, Hughes, L, Ismagilova, E, Aarts, G, Coombs, C, Crick, T, Duan, Y, Dwivedi, R, Edwards, J, Eirug, A, Galanos, V, Ilavarasan, PV, Janssen, M, Jones, P, Kar, AK, Kizgin, H, Kronemann, B, Lal, B, Lucini, B, Medaglia, R, Le Meunier-FitzHugh, K, Le Meunier-FitzHugh, LC, Misra, S, Mogaji, E, Sharma, SK, Singh, JB, Raghavan, V, Raman, R, Rana, NP, Samothrakis, S, Spencer, J, Tamilmani, K, Tubadji, A, Walton, P & Williams, MD (2021) Artificial Intelligence (AI): Multidisciplinary perspectives on emerging challenges, opportunities, and agenda for research, practice and policy. *Int J Inf Manage*, 57, 101994.
[http://dx.doi.org/10.1016/j.ijinfomgt.2019.08.002]

Eling, M & Lehmann, M (2018) The impact of digitalization on the insurance value chain and the insurability of risks. *Geneva Pap Risk Insur Issues Pract*, 43, 359-96.
[http://dx.doi.org/10.1057/s41288-017-0073-0]

Eckert, C & Osterrieder, K (2020) How digitalization affects insurance companies: overview and use cases of digital technologies. *Zeitschrift für die gesamte Versicherungswissenschaft*, 109, 333-60.

Foss, NJ & Saebi, T (2017) Fifteen years of research on business model innovation: How far have we come, and where should we go? *J Manage*, 43, 200-27.
[http://dx.doi.org/10.1177/0149206316675927]

Gartner, (2017) Applying artificial intelligence to drive business transformation: a gartner trend insight report. 2-7.

Guba, EG & Lincoln, YS (1994) Competing paradigms in qualitative research. Handbook of qualitative research. 163-94.

Hair, JF, Black, WC, Babin, BJ & Anderson, RE (2019) *Multivariate Data Analysis. 8th ed Cengage*

Learning, EMEA.

Høgevold, NM, Svensson, G, Wagner, B, Varela, JCS, Ferro, C & Padin, C (2016) Influence of stakeholders and sources when implementing business sustainability practices. *International Journal of Procurement Management,* 9, 146-65.
[http://dx.doi.org/10.1504/IJPM.2016.075261]

Hu, Q, Lu, Y, Pan, Z, Gong, Y & Yang, Z (2021) Can AI artifacts influence human cognition? The effects of artificial autonomy in intelligent personal assistants. *Int J Inf Manage,* 56, 102250.
[http://dx.doi.org/10.1016/j.ijinfomgt.2020.102250]

Jerab, DA, Alper, M & Baslar, A (2011) The impact of core competencies on competitive advantages & success in Istanbul tourists companies. *SSRN,* 1813163.
[http://dx.doi.org/10.2139/ssrn.1813163]

Joram, MK, Harrison, BK & Joseph, KN (2017) A knowledge-based system for life insurance underwriting. *International Journal of Information Technology and Computer Science,* 9, 40-9.
[http://dx.doi.org/10.5815/ijitcs.2017.03.05]

Leedy, PD & Ormrod, JE (2015) *Practical research: planning and design* Pearson publishing, New Jersey.

Lesage, L, Deaconu, M, Lejay, A, Meira, JA, Nichil, G & State, R (2020) A recommendation system for car insurance. *Eur Actuar J,* 10, 377-98.
[http://dx.doi.org/10.1007/s13385-020-00236-z]

Levine, DM, Szabat, KA & Stephan, DF (2015) Business statistics - A first course. Pearson, New York.

Liao, Y, Deschamps, F, Loures, EFR & Ramos, LFP (2017) Past, present and future of Industry 4.0 - a systematic literature review and research agenda proposal. *Int J Prod Res,* 55, 3609-29.
[http://dx.doi.org/10.1080/00207543.2017.1308576]

Malhotra, Y (2001) Expert systems for knowledge management: Crossing the chasm between information processing and sense making. *Expert Syst Appl,* 20, 7-16.
[http://dx.doi.org/10.1016/S0957-4174(00)00045-2]

Mamorobela, S & Buckley, S (2018) Evaluating the effectiveness of social media on knowledge management systems for SMEs. *European Conference on Knowledge Management,* 1064-72.

Mamorobela, SP (2016) Resource-based view model of an expert system for knowledge sharing in an SME in GAUTENG. GBATA2016 Readings Book. Global business and Technology Association.

Mamorobela, SP (2021) Evaluating the effectiveness of social media on knowledge management systems of small, medium and micro enterprises in South Africa. *African Journal of Science, Technology, Innovation and Development,* 1-15.

Mamorobela, SP (2022) Understanding a social media-enabled knowledge management adoption model for small and medium enterprises in south africa: an explanatory sequential mixed methods research design study. *Handbook of Research on Mixed Methods Research in Information Science* IGI Global 324-39.
[http://dx.doi.org/10.4018/978-1-7998-8844-4.ch016]

Manesh, MF, Pellegrini, MM, Marzi, G & Dabic, M (2020) Knowledge in the fourth industrial revolution: Mapping the literature and scoping future avenues. *IEEE Trans Eng Manage,* 68, 1-7.

Marsh, K & Fayek, AR (2010) SuretyAssist: Fuzzy expert system to assist surety underwriters in evaluating construction contractors for bonding. *J Constr Eng Manage,* 136, 1219-26.
[http://dx.doi.org/10.1061/(ASCE)CO.1943-7862.0000224]

Matt, C, Hess, T & Benlian, A (2015) Digital transformation strategies. *Bus Inf Syst Eng,* 57, 339-43.
[http://dx.doi.org/10.1007/s12599-015-0401-5]

Motjolopane, I & Ruhode, E (2021) Factors driving business model innovation in sample case studies in South Africa. *Afr J Sci Technol Innov Dev,* 1-15.

Motjolopane, I, Owolawi, PA & Ruhode, E (2023) *Navigating Business Model Innovation in Small Medium*

Enterprises. Available from: https://benthambooks.com/future-books-by-subject/business-and-economics-and-finance-and-accounting/

Ngulube, P (2020) The movement of mixed methods research and the role of information science professionals. *Handbook of research on connecting research methods for information science research* IGI Global 425-55.
[http://dx.doi.org/10.4018/978-1-7998-1471-9.ch022]

Ngulube, P (2022) Using simple and complex mixed methods research designs to understand research in information science.*Handbook of research on mixed methods research in information science* IGI Global 20-46.
[http://dx.doi.org/10.4018/978-1-7998-8844-4.ch002]

Nowell, LS, Norris, JM, White, DE & Moules, NJ (2017) Thematical analysis: Striving to meet the trustworthiness criteria. *Int J Qual Methods,* 16, 1-13.
[http://dx.doi.org/10.1177/1609406917733847]

Nuruzzaman, M & Hussain, OK (2020) IntelliBot: A Dialogue-based chatbot for the insurance industry. *Knowl Base Syst,* 196, 105810.
[http://dx.doi.org/10.1016/j.knosys.2020.105810]

O'Brien, JA & Marakas, GM (2008) *Management Information Systems.* McGraw-Hill Inc..

Olarewaju, OM & Msomi, TS (2021) Intellectual capital and financial performance of South African development community's general insurance companies. *Heliyon,* 7, e06712.
[http://dx.doi.org/10.1016/j.heliyon.2021.e06712] [PMID: 33898832]

Onwuegbuzie, AJ & Collins, KM (2007) A typology of mixed methods sampling designs in social science research. *Qual Rep,* 12, 281-316.

Pallant, J (2016) *SPSS survival manual: A step by step guide to data analysis using IBM SPSS* McGraw-Hill Education, New York.

Rajagopaul, A, Magwentshu, N & Kalidas, S (2020) *How South African SMEs can survive and thrive post COVID-19.* Providing the Right Support to Enable SME Growth Now and Beyond the Crisis.

Ravitch, SM & Riggan, M (2016) Reason & rigor: How conceptual frameworks guide research. Sage Publications, London.

Rawat, S, Rawat, A, Kumar, D & Sabitha, AS (2021) Application of machine learning and data visualization techniques for decision support in the insurance sector. *International Journal of Information Management Data Insights,* 1, 100012.
[http://dx.doi.org/10.1016/j.jjimei.2021.100012]

Robinson, SM (2008) Understanding the resource-based view: Implications of methodological choices and a new creative context. *Thesis Queensland University of Technology.*

Sachan, S, Yang, JB, Xu, DL, Benavides, DE & Li, Y (2020) An explainable AI decision-support-system to automate loan underwriting. *Expert Syst Appl,* 144, 113100.
[http://dx.doi.org/10.1016/j.eswa.2019.113100]

Santoso, CB, Prabowo, H, Warnars, HLHS & Fajar, AN (2021) Smart Insurance System Model Concept for Marine Cargo Business. *2021 International Conference on Data Science and Its Applications (ICoDSA),* 281-6. IEEE.
[http://dx.doi.org/10.1109/ICoDSA53588.2021.9617499]

Saunders, MN, Lewis, P & Thornhill, A (2009) Research Onion.*Research Methods for Business Students* Pearson Education, United Kingdom.

Simmon, MK (2011) Dissertation and scholarly research: Recipes for success. Available from: http://www.dissertationrecipes.com/ (Accessed on 15/06/2022).

Teddlie, C, Johnson, RB & Tashakkori, A (2021) Foundations of mixed research: Integrating qualitative and quantitative techniques in the social and behavioral sciences. Sage.

Theinnovationhub (2019) The innovation hub management company. Available from: http://www.theinnovationhub.com/

CHAPTER 6

Factors Affecting the Adoption of Data as a Service (DaaS) in Small, Medium, and Micro Enterprises (SMMEs)

Megan Morta[1] and **Osden Jokonya**[1,*]

[1] *Department of Information Systems, Faculty of Economics and Management Sciences, University of the Western Cape, Cape Town, South Africa*

Abstract: Although there are several benefits to the adoption of emerging technologies by Small, Medium, and Micro Enterprises (SMMEs), not many studies have been performed on inhibiting Data as a Service (DaaS) (adoption in SMMEs). This study, therefore, explores Data as a Service (DaaS) adoption factors in Small, Medium, and Micro Enterprises (SMMEs). The study adopted a systematic literature review and TOE framework as a lens to explore the possible factors. The study results suggest that within the technological context, the complexity, network bandwidth, and availability were considered the most important factors that affected the adoption of DaaS in SMMEs. Furthermore, within the organizational context, cost, support, and infrastructure demand were considered the highest factors affecting DaaS adoption in SMMEs. Lastly, within the environmental context, the results indicate that customer demand was considered an environmental factor. In conclusion, the study results suggest that the adoption of DaaS in SMMEs is affected by several TOE factors. Despite limitations associated with convenient sampling and non-empirical data, the study contributes to the body of knowledge on DaaS adoption factors by SMMEs. Further studies may address the mentioned shortcomings by using empirical data.

Keywords: Big data, Data as a service (DaaS), Digital transformation, Everything as a service (XaaS), ICTs, SMMEs, TOE framework.

INTRODUCTION

Digital transformation has been around for nearly 30 years, becoming popular in the late 1990s and then gaining popularity again in the mid-2000s. Digital transformation is seen as an attempt to integrate emerging technologies into business processes for economic benefit. Developments in digital technologies have undoubtedly steered businesses in the direction of embracing the 4th

* **Corresponding author Osden Jokonya:** Department of Information Systems, Faculty of Economics and Management Sciences, University of the Western Cape, Cape Town, South Africa; Tel: 021 959 3522; E-mail: ojokonya@uwc.ac.za

Ignitia Motjolopane, Ephias Ruhode and Pius Adewale Owolawi (Eds.)

industry technologies. These emerging technologies change businesses' operations, resulting in new digital transformation strategies (Verma & Bhattacharyya, 2017). Verma & Bhattacharyya, (2017) said "Digital technologies are rapidly changing, and enterprises adopting these emerging technologies can reduce costs, enhance efficiencies in their business processes, retain customers, and maintain a competitive advantage over their competitors". Although there are many benefits of emerging technologies for SMMEs in SA, within the era of 4IR, many organizations still need to be fully equipped to implement these emerging technologies. Businesses face several challenges when trying to adopt these emerging technologies (Verma & Bhattacharyya, 2017).

Even though emerging technologies have recently become more affordable for businesses to adopt, the degree of adoption amongst South African SMMEs has proved to be rather slow. The lack of resources for the SMMEs sector makes the adoption rate relatively low compared to large businesses in other emerging economies (Wessels & Jokonya, 2022; Zide & Jokonya, 2022). This results in the SMME sector not realizing the benefits of adopting emerging technologies in their business operations. The emergence of new business model innovations such as Everything-as-a-service (XaaS) has narrowed the challenges of SMMES, who do not have adequate resources for digital transformation in their organization. The upsurge of XaaS platforms has made the procurement of digital technology affordable. Yeboah-Boateng and Essandoh (2014), said "These platforms create efficiencies, do not require functional staff, reduce operations and hardware costs, and do not require in-house experts, and technology infrastructure".

Everything-as-a-service (XaaS) platforms are inexpensive because they are built off a pay-as-you-go service (Wessels & Jokonya, 2022; Zide & Jokonya, 2022). One such example of the Everything as a Service (XaaS) is the Data as a Service (DaaS) business model, where SMMES outsource the service to service providers instead of having it in-house. The study's main objective is to explore the factors affecting the adoption of DaaS in small, medium, and micro-enterprise (SMMES). The rest of the chapter is structured as follows: section 2 covers the literature review, Section 3 discusses the research methodology, section 4 presents the study results, and lastly, section 5 discusses the study results and provides a conclusion.

LITERATURE REVIEW

The advent of digital transformation had disrupted several enterprises in such a way that those failing to reinvent and innovate are being faced with extinction. Attaran & Woods (2019) said "Digital transformation is not specifically about Information Technology (IT); it is about redefining your entire business strategy and considering a change to the corporate culture you once knew". Previous studies suggest that for enterprises to survive in the digital era, they need to think of emerging technologies as a strategic competency (Attaran & Woods, 2019; Wessels & Jokonya, 2022). Digital transformation has seen enterprises creating a new business model and using technology as the platform to do so. A good example is the Amazon shopping website which has disrupted the entire concept of shopping and more. Attaran & Woods, (2019) said "In order to survive, enterprises must adapt and take advantage of how the digital world has changed consumer behavior and expectations". Most competitors and customer channels of many enterprises have already gone digital with many customers spending time online searching, reading emails, browsing, and shopping online.

The two major contributors to digital transformation are technology evolution at an exponential rate and data that has become far more usable (Attaran & Woods, 2019; Modisane & Jokonya, 2021). The difference between enterprises' competitiveness and upkeeping is defined by how they are able to master emerging technologies. Digital Transformation is different from other eras in not only the importance and volumes of data but also real-time data from different sources. The era has seen enterprises being able to keep data about their supply chain, about their competitors, about their consumers, and about their markets (Verma & Bhattacharyya, 2017; Wessels & Jokonya, 2022). The ability of enterprises to use data for critical business decisions is the cornerstone of success in the data economy. It brings intelligent options into the light, enabling businesses to do new things right to create consumer value. On that note, digital transformation has provided an opportunity to level the playing field due to low-cost tools and strategies that enable small, medium, and micro enterprises to compete with bigger enterprises (Verma & Bhattacharyya, 2017; Attaran & Woods, 2019).

Modisane & Jokonya, (2021) said "Small, Medium, and Micro Enterprises (SMMEs) are enterprises owned by one or more individuals, and they play a pivotal role in creating employment opportunities in developing countries". SMMEs contribute 30% to the country's economic growth (Small Enterprise Development Agency, 2016). SMMEs in South Africa employ approximately 10.8 million South Africans, which account for 66% of economic-wide employment. A study conducted by Bowler, Dawood, & Page (2007) showed that 40% of small start-up businesses fail within their first year; the following challenges were highlighted in the study, namely, management skills, lack of funding, and investment in adequate technologies and the associated human resources to run the operation. Unfortunately, SMMEs are discouraged from hiring skilled technical specialists due to a lack of funding, which results in a scenario whereby these small businesses hire candidates with a bit of technical knowledge, but not enough expertise (Mohamed & Weber, 2019; Modisane &

Jokonya, 2021). The lack of funding for these small businesses has shown great weakness. The lack of adequate Information and Communication Technology (ICT) skills is a great challenge affecting these small businesses. Therefore, XaaS is beneficial as it offers rental services to perform the tasks required by these SMMEs (Modisane & Jokonya 2021).

Big Data Adoption by SMMEs

Data has become so easily accessible in our world today, and SMMEs can invest in smart devices to gain access to various search engines. Big Data is used to define the large amount of data found on platforms like social media posts, etc. (Mohamed & Weber, 2019; Wessel, Zide, 2022). According to Wessels & Jokonya (2022), big data refers to "the high volume, velocity, and variety of information assets that require processing to provide unique insights that influence strategic decision-making and business process optimization". The effective use of this Big Data can assist SMMEs in maintaining a competitive advantage. According to Zide & Jokonya (2022), data has altered the competition in organizations by enabling innovation and changing business processes. Webb, Maynard, Ahmad & Shanks (2014) reported that technology and innovation are the leading strategies prioritized by SMMEs to achieve growth, influenced by insights gained through using data. SMMEs are using emerging technologies to identify patterns, and trends in the markets and understand customer behavior. Sen, Ozturk, & Vayvay (2016) further concur that SMMEs use data to increase their performance, efficiency, and their ability to make better decisions.

Even though many advantages for small businesses have been realized through the emergence of Big Data, SMMEs in developing economies are still struggling to adopt emerging technologies compared to similar-sized businesses in developed economies (Selamat, Prakoonwit, Sahandi, & Khan, 2019). Previous studies suggest that the adoption of emerging technologies by SMMEs in developing countries comes with its challenges and complexities. Webb, Maynard, Ahmad & Shanks (2014) states that the most key challenges for the adoption of emerging technologies within SMMEs are namely; concerns of giving over the control of data as a whole; this refers to giving up the control of resources to service providers outside of the business, this type of control directly impacts the security and data privacy of the business information and that of their clients (Modisane & Jokonya, 2021). Secondly, vendor lock-in and failures have been raised as a concern, in that there are no standards/norms for cloud computing; literature has noted that switching service providers is not as easy as an organization would hope for because portability between service providers is not seamless (Modisane & Jokonya, 2021). Thirdly, reliability is of great importance to SMMEs using cloud services; this speaks to the uptime of data centers, mobile applications, and websites (Mohamed & Weber, 2019; Modisane & Jokonya, 2021). Lastly, is the issue of the lack of funding to optimally equip the business with the required human resources to carry out the operation (Shah, Soriano & Coutroubis, 2017).

Data as a Service (DaaS)

Zide & Jokonya (2022), said, "Everything-as-a-Service (XaaS) is a term for the wide variability of services and applications emerging for users to access on-demand over the internet instead of being utilized via on-premises means". Everything-as-a-Service facilitates the flexibility for users and enterprises to customize their computing requirements as they desire. Everything-as-a-Service depends on reliable internet connectivity and strong cloud service platforms to gain acceptance among individuals and enterprises (Mohamed & Weber, 2019; Zide & Jokonya, 2022). Modisane & Jokonya, (2021) said, "Data as a Service is an element of XaaS that offers centralized storage for enterprises with various data sources". Zide & Jokonya (2022) said "Information management experts believe that as more enterprises figure out which data assets they can rent for competitive advantage, the DaaS market will continue to expand". Data as a Service is seen as the foundation for both big data analytics and business intelligence markets in enterprises. Previous studies predict a market growth of DaaS as more enterprises start seeing DaaS as the future in the data economy (Zide & Jokonya, 2022; Modisane & Jokonya, 2021).

According to Wessels & Jokonya (2022), "data to this century is what oil was to the last century", therefore, the storage and supervision of data should be equally important. Wessels & Jokonya (2022), state that, lack of data management skills, resources, and knowledge are three key factors that affect the adoption of DaaS in SMMEs. The literature review has provided some evidence that adopting DaaS within SMMEs can provide a competitive advantage. The literature suggests that DaaS solutions adoption in enterprises has been slower compared to other cloud-based solutions.(Zide & Jokonya, 2022, Wessels & Jokonya, 2022). However, more enterprises are expected to leverage the benefits of DaaS as the cloud is becoming increasingly central to modern business operations. SMMEs that choose to adopt DaaS will not require to depend on internal experts to manage and protect their data allowing them to focus on their core business functions (Mohamed & Weber, 2019; Wessels & Jokonya, 2022).

Theoretical Frameworks

The study adopted the Technology -Organisation- Environment (TOE) Framework to explore DaaS adoption factors in SMMEs (Tornatzky and Fleischer, 1990). The Framework states that three main contexts are technological, organizational, and environmental, influencing the decision of technology adoption in organisations. The TOE framework is a suitable theoretical framework for this research study. The TOE framework is strongly aligned with the Information Systems field compared to other adoption frameworks (Yoon & George, 2013). The availability of technologies, both internal and external to the enterprise which might be useful in enhancing the organization's productivity is important to consider from a technological context perspective (Tornatzky & Fleischer, 1990).

The organizational context considers certain shortfalls, such as budget constraints and the resources to employ human capital, SMMEs staying within budget is always critical. The environmental context is the setting in which the organization finds itself; for SMMEs, an example is Government regulations such as the POPI Act and Cyber Security Compliance. SMMEs are required to adhere to these regulations; non-adherence may result in fines being imposed on the enterprise. All these three contexts are posited to influence technological innovation (Fig. **1**).

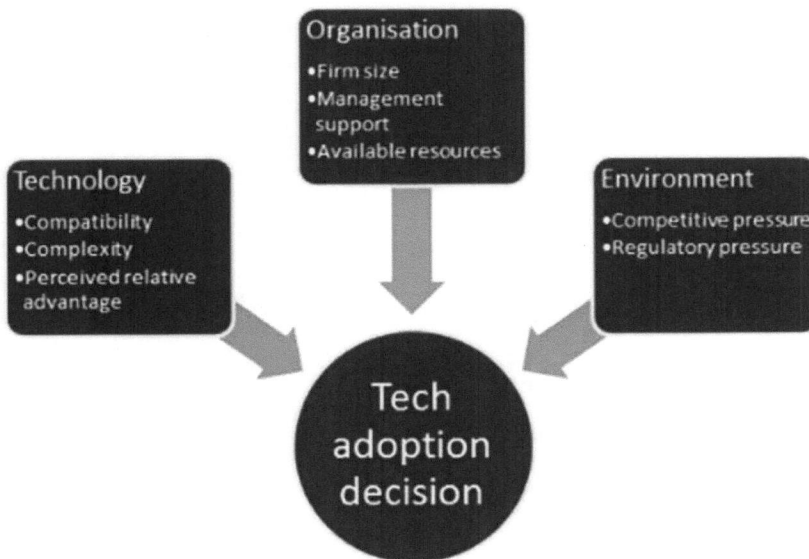

Fig. (1). The Technology, Organisation, and Environment framework (Tornatzky & Fleischer 1990).

Technology Context

The technological context includes all of the technologies that apply to the business; these are both technologies currently used by the firm and those available in the market but not in use. Baker, (2011) said, "The current technologies within the firm remain important in the adoption process as they limit the scope and pace of technological change that the firm can undertake". The technology context's main focus is to study how existing technology features can drive adoption in the business (Tornatzky & Fleisher, 1990). These technological factors usually include cost, scalability, complexity, availability, and security (Ngah, Zainuddin, & Thursamy, 2017).

Organizational Context

Baker(2011) said, "The organizational context refers to the features and resources of the business, including but not limited to linking structures between staff members, firm size, intra-organizational communication processes, firm size, and the number of available resources". The organizational context has been designed to identify its connection to the technology adoption in enterprises. According to Low & Kularatne (2011), the main features of an organization, such as values, skills, structure, and support from leadership, all influence technology adoption culture.

Environment Context

The environmental context of this framework was designed to study features such as the structure of the industry in which the business operates in the absence or presence of technology service providers, and government regulations (Baker, 2011). Tornatzky & Fleisher (1990) said that "the environmental context concentrates on all external factors, such as external stakeholders, government regulations, competition, and the ability to access external resources, which can influence innovation within an enterprise". The next chapter discusses the research methodology used for the study.

RESEARCH METHODOLOGY

The study adopted a systematic literature review and a content analysis research design to explore Data as a Service (DaaS) adoption factor in SMMEs. A systematic literature review allows the researcher to comprehensively and systematically identify and evaluate the current literature in the field (Fink, 2005). The study objective was to explore Data as a Service (DaaS) adoption factor in small, medium, and micro enterprises (SMMEs). The content analysis research design is appropriate to explore DaaS adoption factor by SMMEs. Jokonya, (2015) said, "Content analysis is a research method used to identify patterns in recorded communication". Content analysis involves systematically collecting text data from various sources and forms which may include visual, oral, or written (Jokonya, 2015; Bengtsson, 2016). Content analysis data can be analyzed qualitatively or quantitively, depending on the study objective. This study used quantitative content analysis to analyze the collected data from different literature sources.

Research Instrument

The study used a content analysis matrix which is the design tool used for quantitative content analysis. A content analysis matrix is a tool to show connections between existing research articles to specific aspects of the topic (Bengtsson, 2016). A content analysis matrix tool was used to explore DaaS adoption factors by SMMEs. The content analysis matrix was used to identify factors in the existing literature. A literature search was conducted to explore (DaaS) adoption factors in SMMEs in published articles using the following keywords: "Digital Transformation," "Data-as-a-Service Adoption," "Big Data," and "Technology Organisational- Environment Framework." A total of 40 related articles published during the period 2009-2020 were selected for the study. These articles were manually coded using Microsoft Excel. The content was categorized as shown in Table 1 below; this was done to transform the qualitative data into quantitative data for quantitative analysis.

Data Sources and Sampling

Content analysis accommodates both quantitative (numeric-orientated data) and qualitative (text-based data). In both cases, one categorizes or "codes" words used to transform the data for analysis to deduce the results (Jokonya, 2015; Bengtsson, 2016). Qualitative content analysis, which is mainly text-based data is normally presented in the form of words and themes, in order to interpret the study results (Bengtsson, 2016). The data for the study was gathered from academic search engines. Convenient sampling was used to identify the relevant articles. The sampling method included searching for keywords relevant to the study in various scientific databases such as ResearchGate, IEEE, Elsevier, Sage Publications, Springer, and Google Scholar. The databases were queried, and the search terms such as "factors affecting the adoption of Data-as-a-Service in SMMEs," "technological factors affecting the adoption of Data-as-a-service," and keywords inclusive of "Digital Transformation", "Big Data" and "Technology-Organisational-Environment Framework". The relevant articles for the research topic were selected from the search results returned.

Table 1. TOE factors that influence the adoption of Emerging Technologies for SMMEs

Technology Factors	Organizational Factors	Environmental Factors
Network bandwidth	Management	Competition Support
Relative advantage	Firm size	Government regulations
Compatibility	Support	Customer demand
Availability	Cost	External pressure
Complexity	Infrastructure	Competition
Security	Fear of change	-
-	Employee skills	-

Research Method and Data Analysis

The study adopted the quantitative research method. The quantitative study was found suitable to explore DaaS adoption factors in SMMEs. Convenient sampling was adopted to collect data from different sources such as search engines of selected scientific databases. The collected qualitative data was coded to be analysed quantitatively (Jokonya, 2015). The data collected was organized, and coded using the literature review matrix. The quantitative content analysis was adopted to analyze the collected data to understand DaaS adoption challenges in SMMEs. Data analysis involved categorizing the qualitative data gathered before the data was converted into quantitative data, which was analyzed to produce different statistics.

RESEARCH RESULTS

This section presents the results of the study of DaaS adoption factors in SMMEs selected from 40 articles published from 2009 to 2020. The next sub-section presents the frequencies of demographic data on Data as a Service (DaaS) adoption factors in SMMEs, published from 2009 to 2020. The next sub-section presents the frequencies results of Technology, Organizational, and Environmental framework (TOE) factors that affect Data-as-a-Service (DaaS) in Small, Medium, and Micro Enterprises (SMMEs).

Demographic Data

This sub-section presents the frequencies of demographic data on Data as a Service (DaaS) adoption factors in SMMEs published during 2009-2020. The demographic variable includes publication year, publication region, publication research method, research type, and framework used for the study on Data as a Service (DaaS) adoption factors in SMMEs, which were published from 2009-2020.

Articles Published by Year

Fig. (**2**) below presents the frequency of articles published by region, based on DaaS adoption factors in SMMEs, published during the period 2009-2020 by year. The results show that there was an increase in publications from 2009 to 2020. There was a substantial increase in 2012 followed by 2018 on DaaS adoption factors in SMMEs, published during the period 2009-2020 by year.

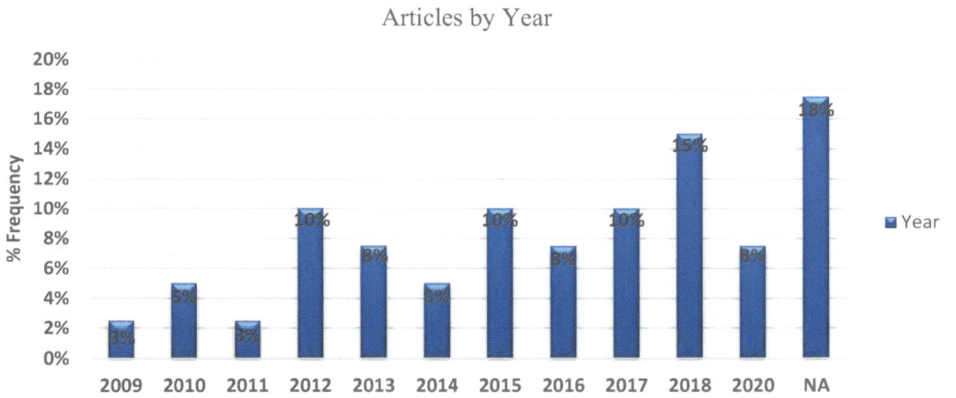

Fig. (2). Articles illustrated by year.

Articles by Region

Fig. (**3**) below presents the frequency of articles published by region, based on DaaS adoption factors in SMMEs, published during the period 2009- 2020 by region. The results show that North America and Europe had the highest recorded number of published articles being 25.00%, respectively, with Asia closely peaking at 20.00%. South America, Africa, and Australia contributed 5.00%, respectively. The frequency shows that North America and Europe account for nearly half of all research based on DaaS adoption factors in SMMEs, published from 2009-2020.

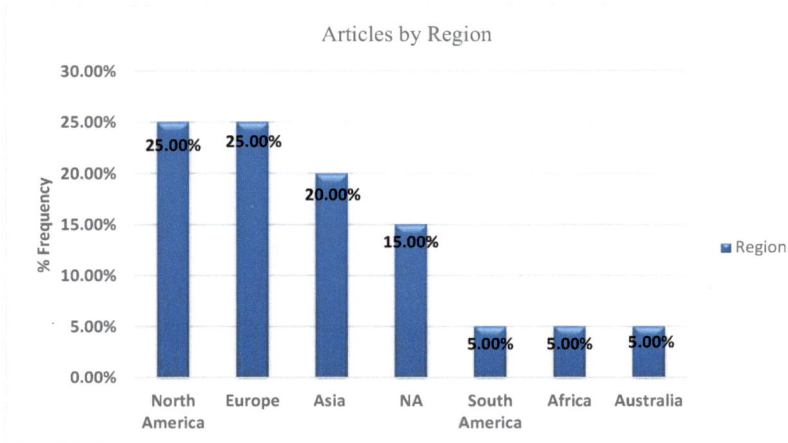

Fig. (3). Articles illustrated by Region.

Articles by Research Method

Fig. **(4)** presents the frequency of research methods used in published articles on DaaS adoption factors in SMMEs, published from 2009-2020. The results show that most of the published articles adopted a qualitative research method. 57.50%, and 42.50% of the published articles adopted a quantitative research method. The results indicate that qualitative research studies were the most used research method on DaaS adoption factors in SMEs in articles published during the period 2009- 2020.

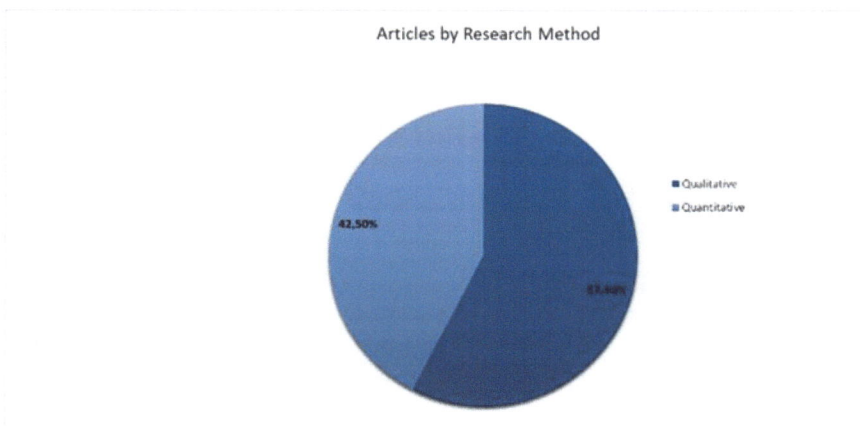

Fig. (4). Articles by Research Method.

Articles by Research Type

Fig. **(5)** presents the frequencies of research-type articles published from 2009-2020 on DaaS adoption factors in SMMEs. The results indicate that most articles published during 2009-2020 conducted 35.00% case studies and experiments were closely 32.50%. The results demonstrate that literature reviews were the third most chosen research method being 12.50%, followed by 10-fold cross-validation types 7.50%.

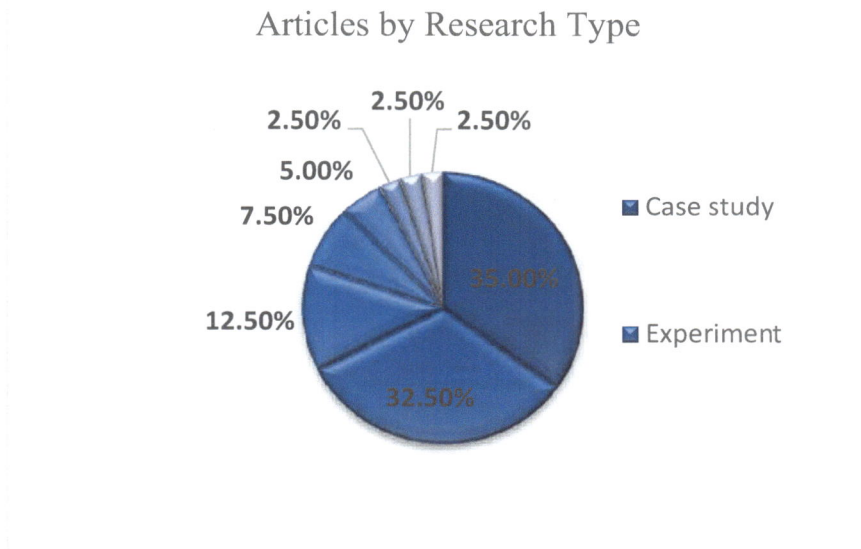

Articles by Research Type

Fig. (5). Articles by Research Type.

Articles by Framework

Fig. **(6)** represents the frequencies of the research frameworks used in articles published from 2009-2020 on DaaS adoption factors in SMMEs. The frameworks used for these studies were the data-mash up optimization, pull QoD evaluation model for DaaS, marketplace repository scaling, the open group architecture framework, DaaS governance framework, data as a service platform, cost-based concurrency control (CCC), and further newer frameworks. NA (not applicable) represents the studies that did not use a framework or develop their framework. The results indicate that most articles, at 35%, did not adopt a framework or recommend a new framework (NA). Additionally, the results demonstrate that the data-mashup-optimization framework was the second most popular among the 7.50% of studies reviewed. All the other frameworks, namely: the pull QoD evaluation model for DaaS, marketplace repository scaling, the open group architecture framework, DaaS governance framework, Data as a Service Platform, cost-based concurrency control (CCC), DaaS platform, service-based approach, Data as a Service, AES-DaaS model, Data in simulation, multi attributes decision-making and new austrian tunneling method were equally implemented at 2.50%, respectively.

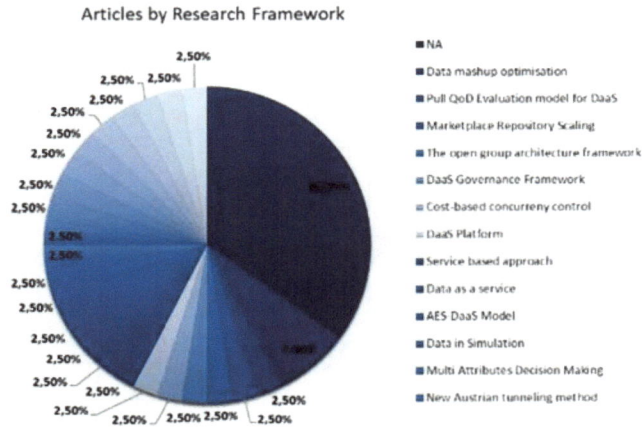

Fig. (6). Articles by Framework.

TOE Factors

This section presents the results of the technology, organizational, and, environmental factors in articles published from 2009-2020 on DaaS adoption factors in SMMEs.

Technological Factors

The study assessed six technology factors that affect the adoption of DaaS by SMMEs which include, complexity, network bandwidth, security, relative advantage, compatibility, and availability. Fig. (7) shows the frequency results of these factors based on the 40 articles that were published during the period 2009-2020. The results indicate that complexity and network bandwidth were considered the highest technology factors that affect the adoption of DaaS by SMMEs. it was referenced in 65% of the 40 articles, followed by availability at 60% and security at 45%. Furthermore, 30% of articles discussed relative advantage as an affecting factor, followed by compatibility at 28% being the least factor listed as an inhibitor for DaaS adoption.

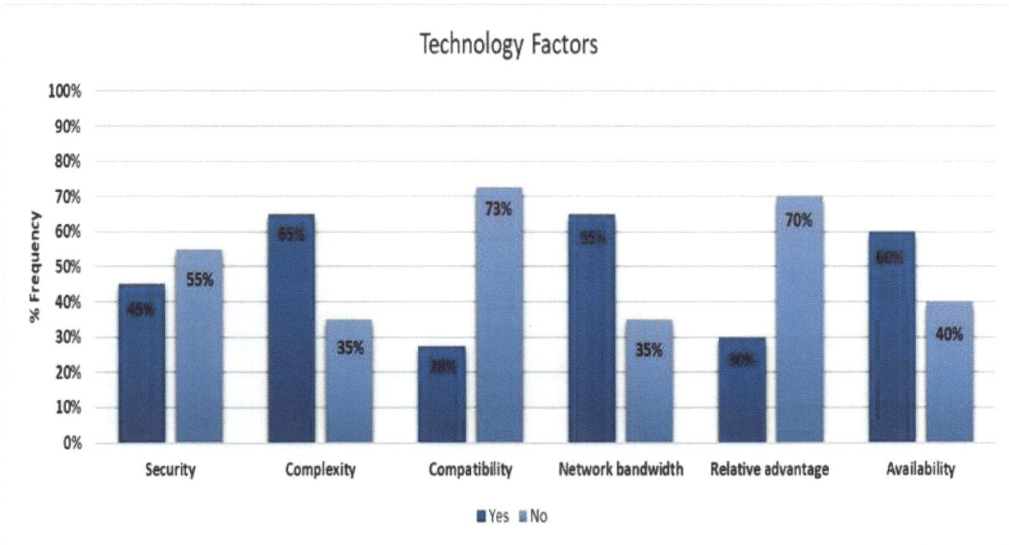

Fig. (7). Frequency of Technology Factors.

Organizational Factors

The study assessed seven DaaS organizational adoption factors that affect SMMEs which include: cost, employee skills, firm size, support, fear of change, infrastructure, and management. Fig. **(8)** shows the results of organizational factors variables based on the 40 articles that were published during the period 2009-2020. The results indicate that cost was considered the highest organizational factor that affected the adoption of DaaS in SMMEs; it was listed in 70% of the 40 articles, followed by infrastructure at 58% and support at 50%. Furthermore, 23% of articles discussed employee skills as an inhibitor, followed by management at 20%. Finally, the fear of change was the least listed factor as it was only cited in 3% of the articles.

Environmental Factors

The study assessed five environmental factors that affect the adoption of DaaS in SMMEs: competition, customer demand, external pressure, government regulations, and support. Fig. **(9)** shows the results of these environmental factors based on the 40 articles published from 2009-2020. The results illustrate that customer demand was the highest listed environmental factor that affected the adoption of DaaS in SMMEs; it appeared in 60% of the 40 articles, followed by government rules and regulations and support at 33% equally, respectively, and external pressure at 28%. Lastly, competition was the least listed factor, as it was only cited in 18% of the articles.

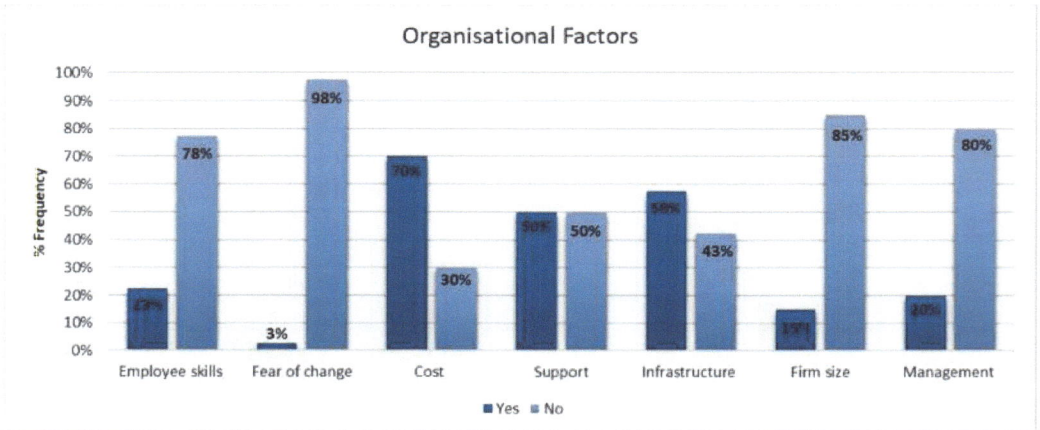

Fig. (8). Frequency of Organisational Factors.

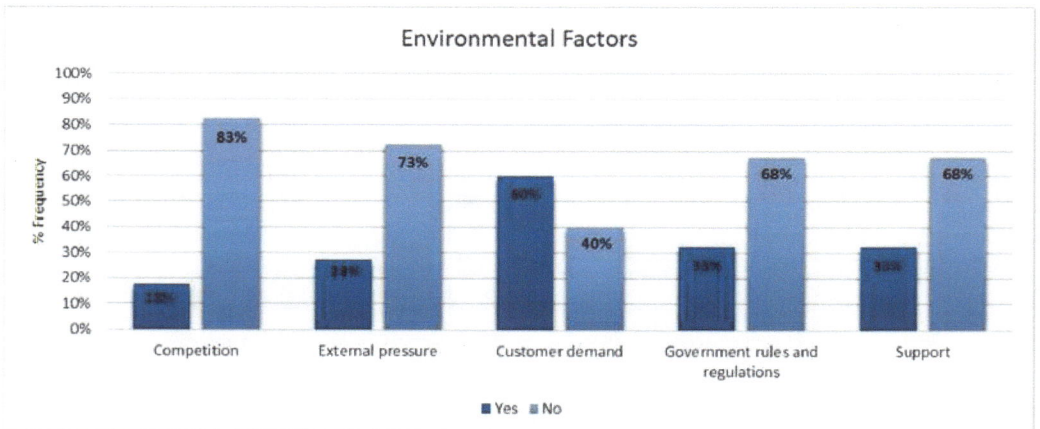

Fig. (9). Frequency of Environmental Factors.

DISCUSSION AND CONCLUSION

The study adopted a systematic review to explore Data-as-a-Service adoption factors in Small, Medium, and Micro Enterprises (SMMEs) on articles published from 2009-2020. The study analyzed 40 published articles on Data-as-a-Service adoption factors in Small, Medium, and Micro Enterprises (SMMEs) from 2017-2020. The study results showed a significant increase in the number of articles published on the DaaS adoption factors in SMMEs. The study results on published further revealed that developed countries like the United States of America, Europe, and Asia; had higher published on DaaS adoption factors in SMMEs compared to the developing countries in regions such as Africa and South America. In addition, the results suggest that qualitative research was the preferred method used in most articles published from 2009-2020.

The study adopted TOE Framework as the theoretical framework to explore the technological, organizational, and environmental DaaS adoption factors in SMMEs. The study results suggest that complexity, network bandwidth, and availability were the most listed technological factors that affected the adoption of DaaS by SMMEs in articles published during the period 2009-2020. Furthermore, cost, support, and infrastructure demand were the most listed organizational factors that affected the adoption of DaaS in SMMEs in articles published during the period 2009-2020. Lastly, the results show that customer demand was the highest listed environmental factor that affected the adoption of DaaS in SMMEs in articles published from 2009-2020, In conclusion, the study aims to explore Data-as-a-Service adoption factors in Small, Medium, and Micro Enterprises (SMMEs). The overall study results suggest the technological (complexity, network bandwidth, and availability), organisational (cost, support, and infrastructure demand), and environmental (customer demand) DaaS adoption factors in Small, Medium, and Micro Enterprises (SMMEs) based on articles published during the period 2009-2020.

The several limitations of the study worth mentioning include the fact that the study data was a non-empirical study based on secondary data. In addition, convenient sampling was also used for the study, which makes it difficult to generalize the study results. Despite the mentioned shortcomings, the study stimulates further studies on Data-as-a-Service adoption factors in Small, Medium, and Micro Enterprises (SMMEs). In addition, the study contributes to the body of knowledge on DaaS adoption factors in Small, Medium, and Micro Enterprises (SMMEs). Further studies may use other research methods to explore the Data-as-a-Service adoption factors in Small, Medium, and Micro Enterprises (SMMEs).

GLOSSARY

- **Academic Search Engines:**   Online platforms that allow researchers to search for scholarly articles and academic publications related to their research topics.
- **Big Data:**   Large volumes of data that require specialized processing to provide insights for strategic decision-making and business process optimization.

- **Business Intelligence:** The use of data analysis tools and techniques to transform raw data into actionable insights for business decision-making.

- **Cloud Computing:** A model for providing on-demand access to a shared pool of computing resources over the internet such as storage, processing power, and applications.

- **Cyber Security Compliance:** The adherence to security standards and practices to protect computer systems networks, and data from cyber threats.

- **Content Analysis:** A research method used to identify patterns and themes in recorded communication involving the systematic collection and analysis of text data from various sources.

- **Convenient Sampling:** A non-probability sampling method in which researchers select the most readily available subjects or data sources for the study.

- **Data as a Service (DaaS):** An element of XaaS that offers centralized storage for enterprises with various data sources. DaaS allows businesses to outsource data services to service providers instead of managing data in-house.

- **Data Management:** The process of organizing storing, protecting, and retrieving data efficiently and securely.

- **Digital Economy:** An economy that is based on digital technologies and the internet including the production and consumption of digital goods and services.

- **Digital Transformation:** The process of integrating emerging technologies into business processes to achieve economic benefits enhance efficiencies, and maintain a competitive advantage over competitors.

- **Enterprise Resource Planning (ERP):** Software systems that integrate various business processes and functions such as accounting, human resources, and inventory management.

- **Everything-as-a-Service (XaaS):** A term that encompasses a wide range of services and applications accessible on-demand over the internet enabling users and enterprises to customize their computing requirements.

- **ICTs:** Information and Communication Technologies which refer to technologies used to process, store, retrieve, transmit, and manipulate information.

- **Information Systems:** The integration of people processes, data, and technology to support decision-making, coordination, control, analysis, and visualization in an organization.

- **Internet of Things (IoT):** A network of interconnected devices embedded with sensors and software that allows them to collect and exchange data over the Internet.

- **POPI Act:** The Protection of Personal Information Act a South African law that regulates the processing of personal information and promotes the protection of individuals' privacy.

- **SMMEs:** Small Medium, and Micro Enterprises, referring to businesses with limited resources and workforce compared to larger corporations.

• **Supply Chain:**   The network of individuals organizations, resources, activities, and technology involved in the production and delivery of goods and services to consumers.

• **Systematic Literature Review:**   A research methodology that involves a comprehensive and systematic review of existing literature on a specific topic to gather relevant information for analysis.

• **Technological Organizational,**   A theoretical framework used to explore factors influencing the
and Environmental (TOE)   adoption of technology in organizations.
Framework:

REFERENCES

Attaran, M & Woods, J (2019) Cloud computing technology: Improving small business performance using the Internet. *J Small Bus Entrep,* 31, 495-519.
[http://dx.doi.org/10.1080/08276331.2018.1466850]

Baker, J (2011) The technology–organization–environment framework. *Information Systems Theory,* 231-45.
[http://dx.doi.org/10.1007/978-1-4419-6108-2_12]

Bengtsson, M (2016) How to plan and perform a qualitative study using content analysis. *NursingPlus Open,* 2, 8-14.
[http://dx.doi.org/10.1016/j.npls.2016.01.001]

Bowler, A, Dawood, MS & Page, S (2007) *Entrepreneurship and Small Business Management.*Juta and Co. Ltd., Pretoria.

Fink, A (2005) *Conducting research literature reviews: From the internet to paper* Sage Publications, Thousand Oaks, California.

Jokonya, O (2015) Investigating open source software in public sector. *Proceedings of the 48th Hawaii International Conference on System Sciences (HICSS 2015)*, January.

Modisane, P & Jokonya, O (2021) Benefits of cloud computing in small, medium, and micro-sized enterprises (SMMES)' *International Conference on ENTERprise Information Systems (CENTRIS 2020) and Project Management (ProjMan 2020), 21st to 23rd October 2020 Vilamoura, Algarve, Portugal.*
[http://dx.doi.org/10.1016/j.procs.2021.01.231]

Mohamed, M & Weber, P (2019) Trends of digitalization and adoption of big data & analytics among UK SMEs : Analysis and lessons drawn from a case study of 53 SMEs.

Selamat, SAM, Prakoonwit, S, Sahandi, R & Khan, W (2019) Big Data and IoT opportunities for small and medium-sized enterprises (SMEs. *In Handbook of Research on Big Data and the IoT* IGI Global. 77-88.

Sen, D, Ozturk, M & Vayvay, O (2016) An overview of big data for growth in SMEs. *Procedia Soc Behav Sci,* 235, 159-67.
[http://dx.doi.org/10.1016/j.sbspro.2016.11.011]

Shah, S, Soriano, CB & Coutroubis, AD (2017) Is big data for everyone? The challenges of big data adoption in SMEs. *2017 IEEE International Conference on Industrial Engineering and Engineering Management (IEEM),* 803-7. IEEE.
[http://dx.doi.org/10.1109/IEEM.2017.8290002]

Small Enterprise Development Agency (2016) *The Small, Medium, and Microenterprise Sector of South Africa.* Commissioned by The Small Enterprise Development Agency.

Tornatzky, LG & Fleischer, M (1990) *The Processes of Technological Innovation.* Lexington Books, Lexington. Van Donk, Verma, S. & Bhattacharyya, S.S. (2017). Perceived strategic value-based adoption of Big Data Analytics in an emerging economy: A qualitative approach for Indian firms. *J Enterp Inf Manag,* 30, 354-82.

[http://dx.doi.org/10.1108/JEIM-10-2015-0099]

Webb, J, Maynard, S, Ahmad, A & Shanks, G (2014) Small and medium enterprises using software as a service: Exploring the different roles of intermediaries. *AJIS Australas J Inf Syst,* 18, 391-404.

Wessels, T & Jokonya, O (2022) Factors affecting the adoption of Big Data as a Service in SMEs, - International Conference on ENTERprise Information Systems, Virtual at Meliá Braga Hotel & SPA, Braga. *Portugal,* 13-5.

Zide, O & Jokonya, O (2022) Factors affecting the adoption of Data Management as a Service (DMaaS) in Small and Medium Enterprises (SMEs) International Conference on ENTERprise Information Systems, Virtual at Meliá Braga Hotel & SPA. *Braga, Portugal,* 13-5.

CHAPTER 7

Factors Affecting the Adoption of Emerging Technologies to Reduce Food Waste by SMEs in the Food Industry

Talent Muzondo[1] and **Osden Jokonya**[1,*]

[1] *Department of Information Systems, Faculty of Economics and Management Sciences, University of the Western Cape, Cape Town, South Africa*

Abstract: Consumers have now been able to purchase whatever food they wish in the 21st century. Not all the food that is purchased is consumed, resulting in food waste. About a third of the food produced is wasted in the world. Humans are the main culprits of food waste. The problem is worsening by each day, with different attempts failing to counter the problem. The study investigates factors affecting the adoption of emerging technologies to reduce food waste by SMEs in the food industry. The TOE framework was used for this purpose. The study adopted a systematic literature review to explore the factors affecting the adoption of emerging technologies to reduce food waste by SMEs in the food industry. The results from the study suggest that complexity, security, usability, cost, and flexibility are important technological factors that affect the adoption of emerging technologies. Furthermore, the results from the study suggest that organisation size and organisation resistance are important organisational factors affecting the adoption of emerging technologies to reduce food waste by SMEs in the food industry. Lastly, the results from the study suggest that IT policy and legislation are important environmental factors affecting this technology adoption. Further studies may consider adopting other research methods to explore factors affecting adopting emerging technologies in reducing food waste by SMEs in the food industry.

Keywords: Digital supply, Emerging technologies, Food waste, Food industry, TOE framework.

INTRODUCTION

Consumers have been able to purchase whatever food they wish in this 21st century. The amount of food bought in stores has increased significantly over the

* **Corresponding author Osden Jokonya:** Department of Information Systems, Faculty of Economics and Management Sciences, University of the Western Cape, Cape Town, South Africa; Tel: 021 959 3522; E-mail: ojokonya@uwc.ac.za

Ignitia Motjolopane, Ephias Ruhode and Pius Adewale Owolawi (Eds.)

past five years (Oelofse & Nahman, 2013: p81). However, this does not mean that the food bought is used accordingly. About a third of food waste comes from the amount of food the consumers buy (Filimonau, Krivcova & Pettit, 2019: p 48). This clearly shows how food waste has become a big problem in the food industry. Food is wasted in all parts of the supply chain. It starts with the production process, where food is wasted due to insufficient equipment. If the harvesting techniques used are not up to standard, it can result in huge amounts of wastage of food (Oelofse & Nahman, 2013: p89). There is wastage of food in storage if the storage facilities are not good enough to preserve the food.

Food is being wasted in all stages of the supply chain. The fact is that food cannot be distributed equally because people have different purchasing powers This makes it difficult to reduce food waste; some buy more than they need and end up throwing it away as it is spoiled (Heikkilä and Juha, 2016: 447). The hunger continues in some areas where people have less money to buy food. It is a big challenge (Aschemann, 2018: 169). Some developing countries are facing food shortage and hunger due to food wastage in other parts of the world. Producers target the people with the money; they do not care about those who cannot afford their products. Food waste plays an important role in reducing hunger in other areas (Filimonau & De Coteau, 2019: 234). If the correct technology is used to reduce food waste, it could benefit those who are less fortunate.

The consumer with higher incomes and increased purchasing power are the biggest culprits of food waste (Loke and Leung, 2015: 1077). They will buy food that they do not need. Unnecessary wastage arises from this. It is mostly experienced in developed countries (Loke and Leung, 2015: 1082). However, in developing countries, it is not the only case; food is also wasted in the development phase due to a lack of proper equipment. The lack of technology in the food industry has increased the amount of food waste, and this trend continues to increase. There is still a gap between the technology available to reduce food waste in the industry and success. This brings the need for emerging technologies that can counter the problem of food waste (Martin-Rios, 2018: 198). The focus is more on food waste in the fast-food industry; the restaurants that provide food as a service. The amount of food wasted in this sector is massive due to the lack of digital technologies that can be used to reduce food waste (Mattila & Mesiranta., 2018: 9). Hence it is an area of interest even though there are other areas where food is wasted in the food industry. Hospitality is another area where food is wasted, but the focus is limited due to the lack of resources for the research required in this sphere. The study objectives were to explore factors affecting the adoption of emerging technologies to reduce food waste by SMEs in the food industry.

LITERATURE REVIEW

History and archaeology believe that people evolved from apes to humans. The theory of evolution for humans could be questioned by many; unfortunately, for technology, it does not seem to be the case. The shift from computers to emerging devices, the automation of computers connecting via wireless devices, and the use of these devices to produce information for humans to use in production and processing are termed industry 4.0 (Tjahjono, 2017: 1176). Approximately 13 billion was invested in digital supply chain technologies in 2017, and an estimated 19 billion is expected to be invested in 2019 (Liddell and Fish, 2018: 6). Industry 4.0 comes with technologies that can be incorporated into the digital supply chain. This technology is more effective in warehouse management, transport logistics, procurement, and order fulfilment functions. However, a collaboration between customers, suppliers, and organizations is critical for the full implementation of industry 4.0 technologies (Berdykulova, 2014). It is beneficial for organizations to implement emerging technologies in the food supply chain. Benefits include increased efficiency, enhanced service levels, improved customer experience, increased responsiveness, high-quality standards, productivity, meeting customer demand and, more importantly, reducing food waste in the SMEs food industry sector.

Food Waste in Food Industry

Food continues to be wasted in all parts of the supply chain. It is in the form of raw or cooked food that is wasted before, during, and after meal preparations in households, as well as in the manufacturing, distribution, retail, and delivery process of the supply chain (Oelofse & Nahman, 2013: 82). It includes food and inedible parts of food removed from the supply chain to be disposed or recovered for example crops planted but not harvested (Aschemann, 2018: 168). According to previous studies, it is estimated that one-third of the food produced is lost or wasted globally, which makes 1.3 billion tonnes per year (Heikkilä, 2016: 451). While another study showed that about one-third of the food is thrown away after consumption.

Food waste continues to be a problematic endeavour causing food insecurity and social inequality. The poor are disadvantaged, while the rich continue to waste food. From an environmental point of view, food waste contributes to the exploitation of natural resources (Richards & Hamilton, 2018: 169). Hunger continues to increase with food not being sufficient to feed the rest. The food and agriculture sector head the top list in damaging the environment. Greenhouse gas emissions released during food preparation also pollute the environment; a study showed that food waste also contributed to water wastage and depleted natural resources (Aschemann, 2018: 172). Developing countries mainly waste food in the production process as they do not have the best technology, while in developed countries, food is wasted in households during consumption (Heikkilä *et al.*, 2016: 453). Minimizing food waste will help increase efficiency and sustainability in the food service sector (Filimonau, Krivcova, & Pettit, 2019: 49). Other related studies have also been performed to reduce food waste in the SMEs food industry.

Related Studies

Numerous attempts have been made to develop a model or framework to reduce it. Several articles found on research conducted to reduce food waste alludes to the point that food waste has become a huge problem globally. There are studies of food waste in general. The focus is to find where exactly the food is wasted in the supply chain. Results show that food is being wasted in all parts of the supply chain, from the production process to the end consumer (Filimonau, Krivcova & Pettit, 2019: 48). Several studies have been conducted to find how food is wasted in developing countries. Many researchers found that more food is being wasted in the production process rather than in households (Martin-Rios *et al.*, 2018: 198). The reason is poor technology found in developing countries to produce efficiently. Finally, there have been several types of research on technologies that can be used to reduce food waste. The technologies, however, focused more on supply chain and barely related to the digital supply chain (Ajay & Ivanov, 2019: 3). The gaps are also identified because there is no link between technologies proposed to the digital supply chain. That is why the gaps need to be filled by using emerging or 4th industrial revolution technologies to reduce food waste.

TOE Framework

The technology-organizational-environmental framework is a framework that is used by many. It helps in driving technology innovation. There are three main constructs of the framework that are: technological factors, organizational factors, and environmental factors. The technological factors focus mainly on the technologies in the industry or the emerging technologies that can be implemented in the industry. The organizational factors focus on the influences that disrupt or interrupt the implementation of the technologies.

Technological Factors

The move to a digital environment allows organizations to use different technologies in their supply chain. Technological factors mainly include products and processes. The focus is, however, more on the processes that organizations use in their supply chain. There have been many technologies that have emerged in today's era. These are called emerging technologies or 4th industrial revolution technologies. Technologies like robotics, 3D and simulation, big data analytics, virtual and augmented realities, drowns, RFID, and IOT are the few that can be implemented in SCM (Cerasis, 2018: 6). These technologies can be implemented in an organization's processes. They are most effective in production, storage, packaging, and delivery. They could be used in different industries, but the focus, however, is on the food industry sector.

Technologies like RFID, sensors and IoT could be used in the packaging and storage of products; for example, RFID is mostly used by organizations to make it easier for them to count stock or inventory (Phase & Mhetre, 2018: 973). While technologies like drowns could be used to deliver food to consumers. If implemented correctly, all the technologies will improve the efficiency of production, enhance customer satisfaction, increase productivity, and reduce food waste by limiting the volume of returns (Liddell & Fish, 2018: 451). Big data analytics also plays a part in the food industry; customer data could be analyzed to give trends and preferences of consumers.

Organizational Factors

Organizational factors also play a part in reducing food waste. There are quite several factors that could be considered, for example, the organization's size. The bigger the organization, the more it is capable of wasting food (Mattila *et al.*, 2018: 4). Big organizations require intensive monitoring and management to avoid wastage of food. Most of the big organizations have their SCM in-house, meaning they do everything for themselves, from production, transportation, and delivery to storage. They have to manage their processes closely as food could be wasted in any of these processes. Other factors include top management support and the availability of financial resources. Investing in the most effective technologies that reduce food waste should be a priority, whether an organization has more or less financial resources (Romani, 2018: 216). The availability of technical skills and the resistance to change also play a part in reducing food waste. If there is resistance to change, it could be difficult to implement new technology in the organization. The top management has to be involved in the production process.

Support from directors is crucial for the implementation of any new technology. Top management provides strategic decisions that can help in making the implementation of new technology easier; for example, employees are more willing to accept change if it is communicated and delivered well by top management (Heikkilä *et al.*, 2016: 449). Top management supports the adoption of technology to reduce food waste. Last but not least, the availability of internal IT resources also affects the adoption of 4th industrial revolution technologies to reduce food waste (Baker, 2018: 11). When there is some presence of IT in the organization, it will be easier to implement other technologies compared to those where there is no presence.

Environmental Factors

Environmental factors are those factors mainly not within the boundary and control of the organization but contribute to food waste. Climatic conditions are at the top of the list as the cause of food waste. A study in South Africa showed that the drought in Cape Town in 2018 increased the amount of food wasted in the food industry (Dreyer, 2019: 506). Government regulations and policies also contribute to food waste. Organizations have to abide by rules and regulations on the quantities they produce. Mostly they produce quantities that are in surplus to the demand to meet government regulations.

Food waste harms the environment itself. The amount of food wasted by the consumer contributes to environmental degradation. Even livestock farming produces significant environmental emissions in the form of methane derived from the enteric fermentation of ruminants. The application of fertilizers creates direct emissions of nitrous oxide from soil processes (Scherhaufer, 2018: 99). These are all hazardous emissions that are harmful to the environment. The goal is to reduce food waste and preventing environmental degradation. The availability of external vendors also can be seen as an environmental factor. The more IT vendors in the market, the better it will be for organizations to access technology to reduce food waste. Most companies fear the excessive budgets that come with implementing new technology in the company (Scherhaufer and Moates, 2018: 100). If they are many suppliers in the industry, it will create competition between these suppliers. They will be forced to lower their prices. Organizations can now buy this technology at much cheaper prices.

Theoretical Framework

The theoretical framework to be used in this study is the Technology-Organisational-Environmental (TOE) framework. The framework helps organizations understand the factors affecting a certain research topic. For this case, the topic was finding out the emerging technologies that can be used to reduce food by SMEs in the food industry. In terms of technology, the framework helps managers and employees access the technology needed in their organizations. It provides a view of what needs to be done and what affects the implementation of the desired technology. The technological factors include security issues, compatibility, usability, availability, and benefits. These are the common factors that influence the technological adoption part of the TOE framework. Organizational factors are those internal factors that affect the adoption of technology. They are usually inbound and can be controlled by the organization. Organizational size, culture, financial position, and top-management support are some of the factors found on the organizational side of the TOE framework. The last part of the TOE framework is the environmental factors. These are the factors that are mainly out of the control of the organizations as they are external. The most common factors are climatic conditions, government regulations, infrastructure, market structure, and IT policy. The level of these factors differs at all times and affects the organizations in different ways. The three factors of the TOE framework affect the implementation of new technology in different ways and levels. It, however, helps in providing a guideline that can be followed to counter the challenges that arise.

RESEARCH METHODOLOGY

The study adopted the systematic literature review to explore factors affecting the adoption of emerging technologies to reduce food waste by SMEs in the food industry. A systematic literature review is an objective-oriented research design that focuses on answering the research question together to meet the objectives (Baird, 2018: 341). It focuses on the explicit inclusion of the literature that is wanted. It is easy to answer research questions by using a systematic review as it focuses on the practical implications of the research question and excludes non-relevant information (Burgers, Brugman & Boeynaems, 2019: 5). It is easy to avoid bias using a systematic literature review if the right keywords are used. The advantage of using a systematic literature review is that other researchers can also update the research at a later date or build from it. That is why, it is the most appropriate choice for this research considering the time factor and the changing technologies in the food industry sector. Certain inclusions and exclusions were considered in terms of the criteria.

Instrument Development

The TOE framework was used to develop the instrument for extracting information from the published articles on factors affecting the adoption of emerging technologies to reduce food waste by SMEs in the food industry, published during the period 2014-2019. The technological, organizational, and environmental factors made it easier to extract information from the literature related to factors affecting the adoption of emerging technologies to reduce food waste by SMEs in the food industry (Table **1**).

Table 1. TOE Framework Constructs.

The TOE Framework		
Technological Factors	**Organisational Factors**	**Environmental Factors**
4th industrial technologies Security issues Compatibility Usability Cost of Adoption Benefits	Financial position Capacity Technical skills Capacity Organisational Size Top management support	Government regulations Climate conditions Infrastructure Market structure IT policy Energy consumption

Data Sources and Sampling

Data Source: Science Direct and Taylor & Francis Journals are the data sources used for this research.

Sampling bias is the challenge faced in doing a systematic literature review. The keywords have to be clearly defined to counter this challenge. If the keywords are known and related to the research question, then sampling bias can be avoided. The inclusion and exclusion criteria help to reduce publication bias where the results found from the research are not justifiable for publication (Karos, Alleva & Peters, 2018: 788). This occurs after the article has been reviewed (Table **2**).

Table 2. Selection Criteria.

Research Instrument and Sampling			
No.	**Criteria**	**Inclusion Criteria**	**Exclusion Criteria**
1	Language of articles	Articles must be in English	Not in English
2	Time Published	Published from 2015 to the beginning of 2019	Articles published before 2015
3	Relation to food waste	Strong relation to food waste in the food industry sector	Weak or no relation to food waste.
4	Type of articles	Peer reviewed	Opinions and no peer review
5	Article methodology	Quantitative	N/A

Research Methods

Scoping -The research question was formulated after identifying the problem in the industry. Food waste continues to be a problem in the food industry sector. The scope is to develop and understand the 4th industrial technologies that can be used to reduce food waste. This research has yet to be done, although there is similar research from the literature that focuses on reducing food waste. The technologies are outdated to this day.

Planning - Keywords for searching the literature are used so that important articles are not neglected. Keywords like digital supply chain, food waste, 4th industrial technologies, TOE, and food industry sector are used to identify the articles that can be used. A selection criterion is used to filter the results and refine them. Language published to date, relation to the research question, and the type of articles form part of the criteria to be used whether to include or exclude an article.

Searching - Two online databases were used to search for the articles. Science Direct and Taylor & Francis journals. The focus is on finding peer-reviewed articles. The filtering mechanisms were used to search for relevant articles.

Screening - A reference manager called Mendeley was used to import citations and results from the online databases. This helped in saving and backing up all results searched for. Eligibility - This is the final stage of the research method. Here only the articles that meet the inclusion criteria are analyzed. Reviewing all text, not just looking at the abstract, is necessary. More emphasis is on information in the body of the article with relevance to the question.

Data Analysis

For the context of this article, data analysis was performed by using existing articles that were peer-reviewed. The data was collected and categorized according to chosen groups of published articles. A selection criterion was used to refine and sort out the relative articles from different journal publishers (Sharma & Francis, 2017: 35). A total of 70 articles were manually coded in an excel sheet and grouped accordingly. The grouping was done in line with the keywords of the researcher used to search for the best and most relevant data. The researcher used cognitive skills to identify the quality of the data in any article, looking at similarities and relevance. Articles were selected according to technological, organizational, and environmental factors that affect food waste in the food industry sector. The focus was on finding reliable articles. Reliability focuses on producing or finding the same results from the same research process. The results have to be consistent for reliability to be proven true (Ellis & Hojlo, 2018: 242). In terms of data analysis, the qualitative data was converted and coded into quantitative data. The data was then analyzed using an analysis tool called PSPPIRE data editor. This was used to identify frequencies related to factors affecting the reduction of food waste in the food industry sector. The correlation between two variables was also used to identify the relationship between variables affecting the reduction of food waste. Finally, one-Way ANOVA post hoc tests were conducted to confirm statistically significant relationships between the TOE variables identified in this study.

STUDY RESULTS

This section presents the results from the analysis of data conducted for the study. The main objective was to find factors affecting the reduction of food waste by SMEs in the food industry sector. The results were based on an analysis of articles collected between 2014 and 2019. The first section presents results on the demographics of the data analyzed. The second section presents the frequencies of the TOE framework (technological, organizational and environmental) constructs obtained from the data analysis. The third section presents the analysis of variance between demographic data and the TOE framework (technological, organizational and environmental) constructs. The last section presents the correlation between the TOE framework (technological, organizational and environmental) constructs obtained from the data analysis.

Articles Published by Year

Fig. (**1**) below illustrates the frequency of articles on factors that affect food waste by SMEs in the food industry sector, published during the period 2014-2019. The results show that 33% of related articles were published during 2014-2017, whereas 67% of related articles were posted later during 2018-2019. These results suggest that there had been a steady increase in research output during 2014-2017; the highest was in 2018, when it was up to 50%. 2019 showed a download percentage. Furthermore, the lowest recorded research output occurred in 2014 to be 4%, whereas the results depict a marked increase in research output during 2018-2019, with the highest research output occurring during 2018.

Articles by Region

Fig. (**2**) shows the results of the frequency of articles on factors that affect food waste by SMEs in the food industry sector, published during 2014-2019 by region. The results show that Europe had the highest recorded number of published articles being 46%, followed by Africa, 19%, and Central America, 13%. Additionally, Central America and Asia had the lowest number of articles jointly published being 9%. The frequency illustrates that Europe accounts for almost half of the articles used for research based on factors that affect food waste by SMEs in the food industry sector. This was obtained from the articles that were published from 2014-2019.

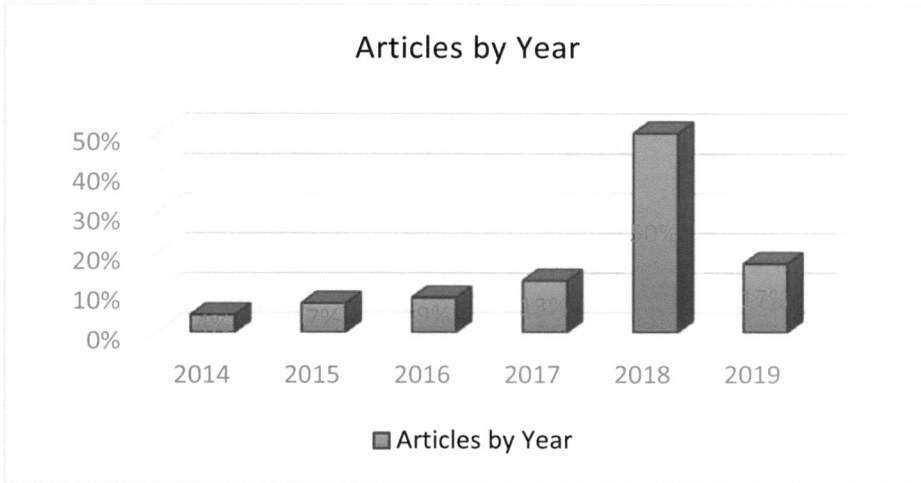

Fig. (1). Articles by year.

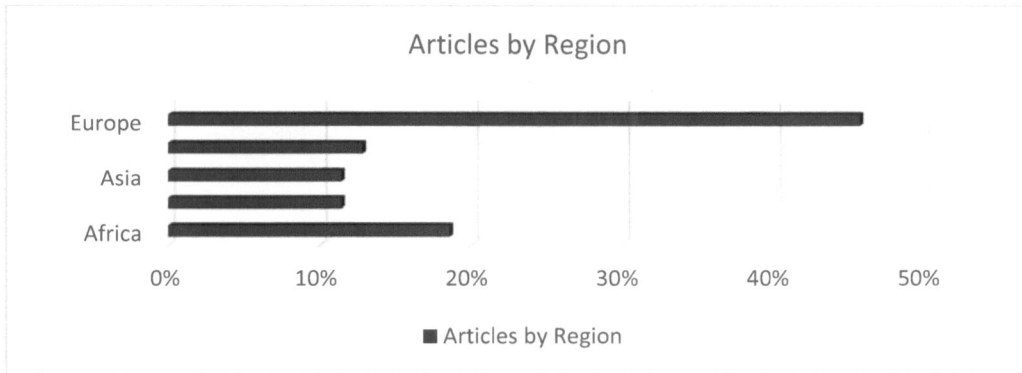

Fig. (2). Articles by Region.

Articles by Research Method

Fig. (3) presents the results of the frequency of the research methods used in articles, based on factors that affect the reduction of food waste by SMEs in the food industry sector, published from 2014-2019. The results showed that most published articles (50%) conducted qualitative research studies, followed by mixed research studies which combined both qualitative and quantitative studies being 26%, and finally, quantitative research studies, with the least frequency of 24%. The results suggest that qualitative research studies were the most used research method based on factors that affect the reduction of food waste by SMEs in the food industry sector.

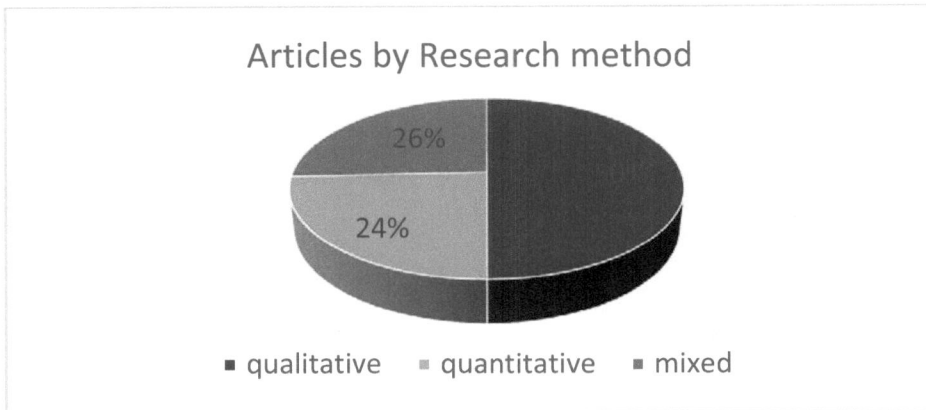

Fig. (3). Articles by Research method.

Articles by Research Type

Fig. **(4)** shows the results found on the frequency of the research types used in articles analyzed, based on factors that affect the reduction of food waste by SMEs in the food industry sector, published during 2014-2019. The results dictated that most articles published during 2014-2019 conducted a survey research-based type being 50%, followed by case studies showing the second majority of 34% and, finally, systematic literature review 16%. Furthermore, the results showed that a systematic literature review was still to be adapted for further research as it had the lowest frequency obtained. This proved that a systematic literature review must be done to produce better results in finding ways that affect the reduction of food waste by SMEs in the food industry sector.

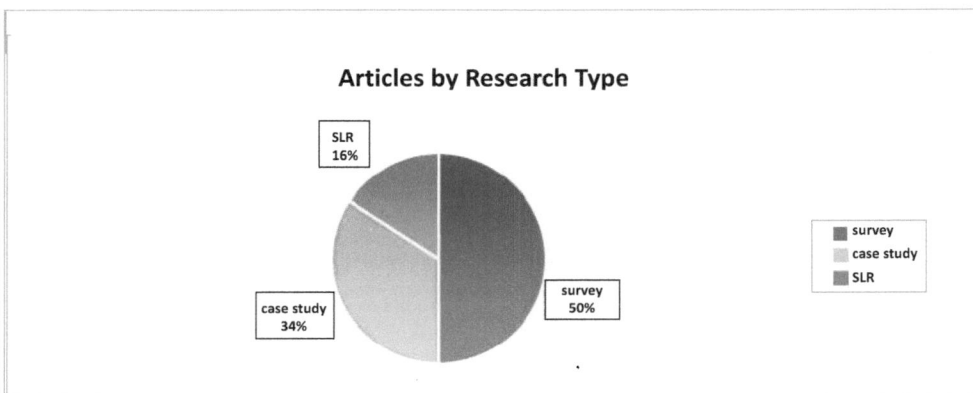

Fig. (4). Articles by Research Type.

Articles by Framework

Fig. (5) below presents the results found from the analysis. The frequencies presented are based on the research frameworks used in articles, on factors affecting the reduction of food waste by SMEs in the food industry sector, published between 2014-2019. It was found that most of the articles analysed did not have a framework used. Therefore, it is depicted by the note applicable notation (N/A); this was 31%. Secondly, the Technology-Organisatio--Environment framework (TOE) was second on the list, with 29%, not far behind NA. The results showed that the conceptual framework was also widely used in the articles. It came third on the list with a similar value to the two above. Finally, the results illustrate that other frameworks had the list frequency. These are frameworks that were not in more than 3 articles. They were combined to represent the "other" as a notation to be considered but not forgotten. These are the findings of the frequencies of frameworks that affect the reduction of food waste by SMEs in the food industry sector.

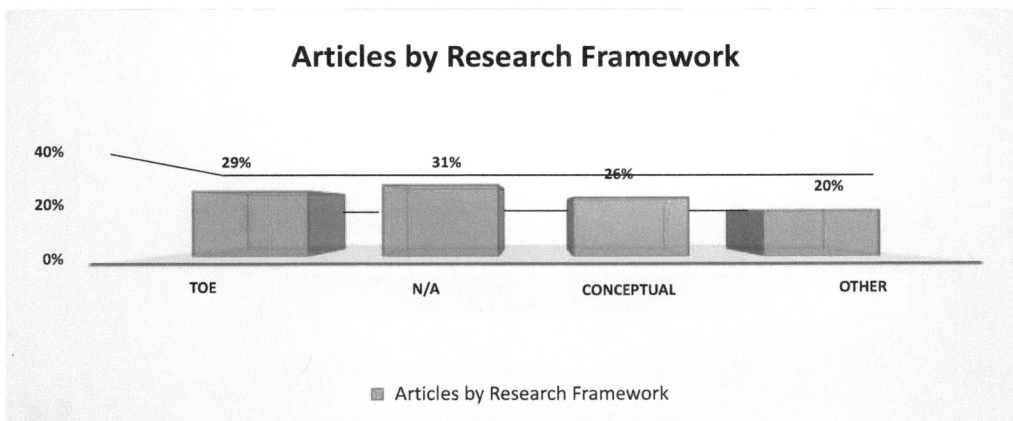

Fig. (5). Articles by Research Framework.

The next sections discuss the frequency of factors affecting the reduction of food waste by SMEs in the food industry sector. This section presents the results from the analysis of the technology, organizational and environmental factors that affect the reduction of food waste by SMEs in the food industry sector.

Technological Factors

The study analysed six factors that affect the reduction of food waste by SMEs in the food industry sector; these included factors such as complexity, security, compatibility, usability, cost, and flexibility. Fig. (**6**) below shows the frequency results on the technological factors based on 70 articles published during the period 2014-2019. The results illustrate that cost was the major factor that affected the use of technological factors to reduce food waste by SMEs in the food industry sector. Compatibility was seen as the highest factor that did not affect the reduction of food waste using emerging technologies. The rest of the factors were relatively similar regarding influence, as we see that security, flexibility, and complexity were in the 50-60% range. Finally, the results showed that technological factors are expensive, and that the challenge makes many companies reluctant to implement them by SMEs in the food industry sector.

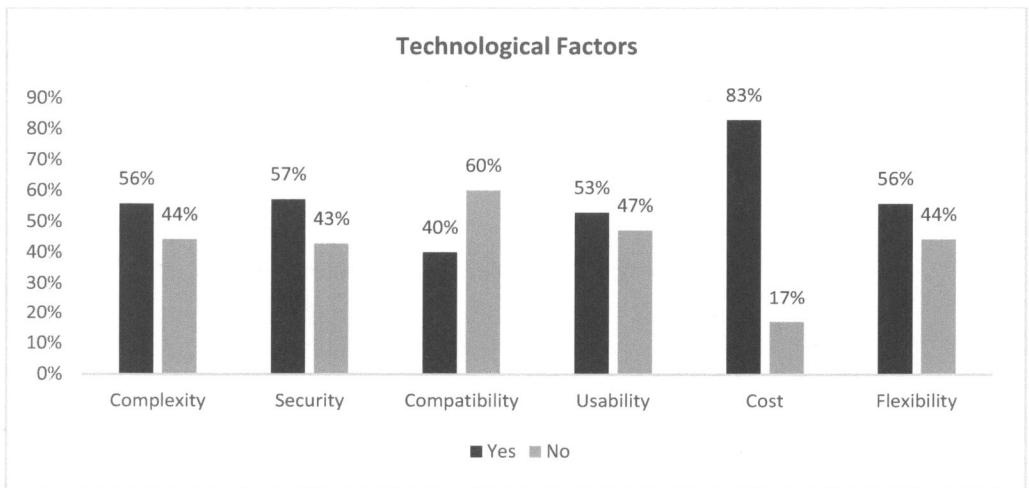

Fig. (6). Technological Factors.

Organizational Factors

Similarly, this research study measured 6 organizational factors that affect the reduction of food waste by SMEs in the food industry sector; these included factors such as organizational size, resistance to change, top management support, technical skills, strategy, and organizational resources. Fig. (**7**) below presents the results obtained from the analysis conducted using the 70 articles from 2014-2019. The results illustrate that the organization's size affected the food waste reduction by SMEs in the food industry sector by a high 76%. Technical skills, the strategy used, and top management support were in the middle with relevant influences. The most surprising with the least percentage was organizational resources which were not mentioned well enough in the articles as a major factor that affect the reduction of food waste by SMEs in the food industry sector, which was 26%.

Fig. (7). Organisational Factors Frequency.

Environmental Factors

This research study measured 6 environmental factors that affect the reduction of food waste by SMEs in the food industry sector; these included factors such as IT policy, climatic conditions, infrastructure, economic environment, energy consumption, and legislation. Fig. (**8**) shows the results analysed based on the environmental factors in the 70 articles from 2014-2019. IT policy was found to be the most relevant factor from the analysed articles that affects the food waste reduction by SMEs in the food industry sector. The range of the other factors, from climatic conditions to energy consumption, was not mentioned as much and fell just under 40%. It is seen that legislation also influenced the reduction of food waste by SMEs in the food industry sector, as it fell just above 55%. Overall the environmental factors did not produce positive results. Only two factors were above 50%, the rest falling under the average cape of 50%.

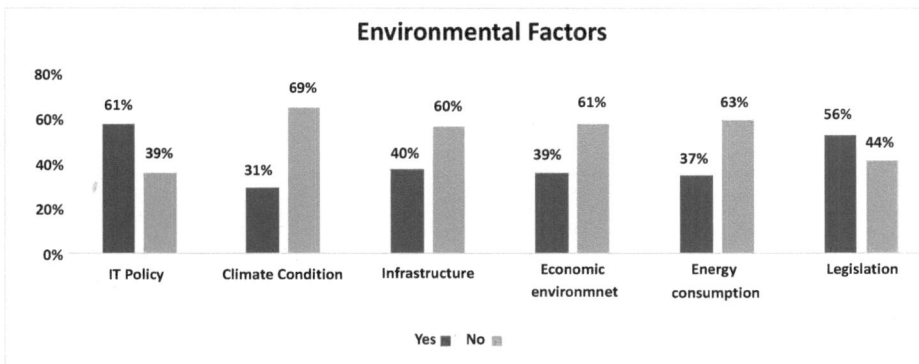

Fig. (8). Environmental Factors Frequencies.

Analysis of Variance (ANOVA) of TOE Construct Variables *vs.* Demographic Variable

This section presents the results from the analysis of variance. The test results are based on different demographic variables, including the year published, the research method used, the research type, the research framework, and the study region. The results presented in this section are only for variables that were tested significantly.

Technological Factors by Region

Table (3) below presents the analysis of the variance (ANOVA) on the variable region and the technology factors (complexity, security, and flexibility)The results showed significance values for the technical factors which are all below 0.05, i.e., complexity at 0.02, compatibility at 0.025, and perceived usefulness at 0.021. This suggests that there is a significant relationship between technology factors (complexity, security, and flexibility) and the demographic variable region. This suggests that there is a relationship between the region's demographic variable and the technological factors (complexity, security, and flexibility) on factors affecting the adoption of emerging technologies to reduce food waste by SMEs in the food industry.

Table 3. Analysis of the variance (ANOVA) on region and the technology factors.

T1._ Complexity	Between Groups	Sum of Squares 3,96	df 4	Mean Square ,99	F 4,84	Sig. ,002
-	Within Groups	13,31	65	,20	-	-
-	Total	17,27	69	-	-	-
T2._ Security	Between Groups	2,65	4	,66	2,99	,025
-	Within Groups	14,17	64	,22	-	-
-	Total	16,81	68	-	-	-
T6._ Flexibility	Between Groups	2,76	4	,69	3,09	,021
-	Within Groups	14,51	65	,22	-	-
-	Total	17,27	69	-	-	-

Organizational Factors by Region

Table (4) below presents the analysis of the variance (ANOVA) on region and the organizational factors (organizational strategy and organizational resources). The results indicate that the significance values for both organizational factors are all above 0.05, i.e., both organizational strategy and organizational resources are

0.125 and 0.115. The results suggest that there is no significant relationship between the organizational factors (organizational strategy/organizational resources and the variable demographic region). They showed no relationship between the organisational factors affecting the adoption of emerging technologies to reduce food waste by SMEs in the food industry and the region the articles analysed collected.

Table 4. Analysis of the variance (ANOVA) on region and the organizational factors.

O5._Strategy	Between Groups	1,72	4	,43	1,88	,125
-	Within Groups	14,87	65	,23	-	-
-	Total	16,59	69	-	-	-
O6._Organisational_Resources	Between Groups	1,42	4	,36	1,94	,115
-	Within Groups	11,95	65	,18	-	-
-	Total	13,37	69	-	-	-

Environmental Factors by Region

In Table (**5**) below shows the analysis of the variance (ANOVA) on region and the environmental factors (climate conditions, infrastructure, and energy consumption) demonstrating that the significance value of climate conditions is at 0.026, which lies below 0.05. Infrastructure is also at 0.041, which is below the significance level. The results suggest that there is a significant relationship between the environmental factors (climate conditions and infrastructure) and the demographic variable of the region. The study results indicate a relationship between the environmental factors affecting the adoption of emerging technologies to reduce food waste by SMEs in the food industry and the published articles regions.

Table 5. Analysis of the variance (ANOVA) on region and the environmental factors.

E2._Climate_Conditions	Between Groups	2,33	4	,58	2,96	,026
-	Within Groups	12,76	65	,20	-	-
-	Total	15,09	69	-	-	-
E5._Infrastructure	Between Groups	2,36	4	,59	2,65	,041
-	Within Groups	14,44	65	-	-	-
-	Total	16,34	69	-	-	-

Correlation Between TOE Factors

Table **6** below shows the correlation between TOE factors which are technological, organisational factors, and environmental factors. Technology and organizational factors had a Pearson correlation of -0.15 (negative value) and, thus indicating a non-significant negative relationship between the two factors. Technology and environmental factors had a negative Pearson correlation of -0.27 thus indicating a non-significant negative relationship between the two factors. However, organizational and environmental factors showed a significant negative correlation of -0.02. This shows that there is a negative relationship between the factors. The value, also shows that the relationship is strong. The results suggest that there is no significant statistical relationship between the technological and organizational factors affecting the adoption of emerging technologies to reduce food waste by SMEs in the food industry.

Table 6. TOE Framework Constructs Correlations.

-		Tech_Tot	Org_Tot	Env_Tot
Tech_Tot	Pearson Correlation Sig. (2-tailed) N	1,00 70	-,15 ,223 70	-,27 ,025 70
Org_Tot	Pearson Correlation Sig. (2-tailed) N	-,15 ,223 70	1,00 70	-,02* ,838 70
Env_Tot	Pearson Correlation Sig. (2-tailed) N	-,27 ,025 70	-,02* ,838 70	1,00 70

*Correlation is significant at the 0.05 level [2-tailed].
*Correlation is significant at the 0.01 level [2-tailed].

DISCUSSION AND CONCLUSION

The study used a systematic literature review to explore the factors that affect the adoption of emerging technologies by SMEs in the food industry. The study results suggest that there was a steady increase in published articles on factors that affect the reduction of food waste by SMEs in the food industry sector during 2014-2018. The highest number of published articles from 2014-2019 on factors that affect the reduction of food waste by SMEs in the food industry sector were from Europe which accounted for nearly fifty percent. The study results suggest most published articles from 2014-2019 on factors that affect the reduction of food waste by SMEs in the food industry sector were based on qualitative methods which accounted for fifty percent of the articles. The study results suggested most published articles from 2014-2019 on factors that affect the reduction of food waste by SMEs in the food industry sector used a surveys research strategy which accounted for fifty percent of the articles. The study results suggest most published articles from 2014-2019 on factors that affect the reduction of food waste by SMEs in the food industry sector did not indicate the research framework or model. However, the Technology-Organisatio--Environment framework (TOE) framework was the most listed, with 29% of the published articles.

The study results suggest that complexity, security, usability, cost and flexibility were the most listed technological factors affecting the adoption of emerging technologies in the reduction of food waste by SMEs in the food industry. The study results suggest that size and resistance were the most listed organisational factors affecting the adoption of emerging technologies in the reduction of food waste by SMEs in the food industry. The study results suggest that IT policy and legislation were the most listed environmental factors affecting the adoption of emerging technologies in reducing food waste by SMEs in the food industry. The study results indicate that technological, organisational and environmental factors affect the adoption of emerging technologies in the reduction of food waste by SMEs in the food industry.

In conclusion, the study results indicate that the TOE factors that affect the adoption of emerging technologies in reducing food waste by SMEs in the food industry. The study had, however, several limitations worth mentioning. The study was not based on empirical data but on secondary data from a systematic literature review. Despite the mentioned shortcomings, the study stimulates further studies on factors that affect the adoption of emerging technologies in the reduction of food waste by SMEs in the food industry. In addition, the study contributes to the body of knowledge on factors affecting the adoption of emerging technologies in the reduction of food waste by SMEs in the food industry. Further studies may consider adopting other research methods to explore factors affecting the adoption of emerging technologies in reducing food waste by SMEs in the food industry.

GLOSSARY

4th Industrial Revolution	Also known as Industry 4.0, it refers to the current era characterized by the integration of advanced digital technologies into industrial processes.
Big Data Analytics	The process of analyzing large and complex datasets to derive valuable insights and patterns for decision-making
Digital Supply Chain	The application of digital technologies and automation in supply chain processes to enhance efficiency and reduce waste.

Digital Technologies	Technologies that rely on digital information and communication, such as computers, smartphones, and internet-based services.
Digital Transformation	The integration of digital technologies into various aspects of business operations to drive innovation and improve efficiency.
Emerging Technologies	Novel and advanced technologies that are relatively new in the market and have the potential to transform industries and processes.
Food Industry	The sector that encompasses the production, processing, packaging, distribution, and consumption of food products.
Food Waste	The food that is discarded and not consumed, leading to a loss of valuable resources and contributing to environmental problems.
IoT (Internet of Things)	A network of physical objects embedded with sensors, software, and connectivity to exchange data and perform actions.
IT Policy	Policies and guidelines set by organizations or governments to govern the use and management of information technology.
IT Vendors	Companies or suppliers that provide information technology products and services to other organizations.
RFID	Radio-Frequency Identification, a technology that uses radio waves to identify and track objects or products.
SMEs (Small and Medium Enterprises)	Small and medium-sized businesses that have limited resources and manpower compared to larger organizations.
Systematic Literature Review	A research methodology that aims to comprehensively and systematically review existing literature on a specific topic.
TOE Framework	Technology-Organizational-Environmental Framework, a theoretical framework used to study the factors influencing the adoption of technology in organizations.

REFERENCES

Aschemann-Witzel, J, de Hooge, IE, Almli, VL & Oostindjer, M (2018) Fine-tuning the fight against food waste. *J Macromark,* 38, 168-84.
[http://dx.doi.org/10.1177/0276146718763251]

Baird, R (2018) Systematic reviews and meta-analytic techniques. *Seminars in Pediatric Surgery,* Elsevier Inc 27, 338-4.
[http://dx.doi.org/10.1053/j.sempedsurg.2018.10.009]

Baker, J (2018) *oo f re ct Pr.* (September 2011).
[http://dx.doi.org/10.1007/978-1-4419-6108-2]

Berdykulova, GMK, Sailov, AIU, Kaliazhdarova, SYK & Berdykulov, EBU (2014) The emerging digital economy: Case of kazakhstan. *Procedia Soc Behav Sci,* 109, 1287-91.
[http://dx.doi.org/10.1016/j.sbspro.2013.12.626]

Burgers, C, Brugman, B C & Boeynaems, A (2019) Systematic literature reviews: Four applications for interdisciplinary research. *ournal of Pragmatics.* Elsevier Ltd.
[http://dx.doi.org/10.1016/j.pragma.2019.04.004]

Cerasis (2018) *'The Digital Supply Chain: The Landscape, Trends, Types, and the Application in Supply Chain Management, A Publication of Cerasis.*

Dreyer, HC, Dukovska-Popovska, I, Yu, Q & Hedenstierna, CP (2019) A ranking method for prioritising retail store food waste based on monetary and environmental impacts. *J Clean Prod,* 210, 505-17. [http://dx.doi.org/10.1016/j.jclepro.2018.11.012]

Ellis, S & Hojlo, J (2018) *Surviving Supply Chain Disruption — Digitally Transforming from Innovation to Execution.*

Filimonau, V & De Coteau, DA (2019) Food waste management in hospitality operations: A critical review. *Tourism Management,* Elsevier, 234-45. [http://dx.doi.org/10.1016/j.tourman.2018.10.009]

Filimonau, V, Krivcova, M & Pettit, F (2019) An exploratory study of managerial approaches to food waste mitigation in coffee shops. *International Journal of Hospitality Management,* Elsevier, 76, 48-57. [http://dx.doi.org/10.1016/j.ijhm.2018.04.010]

Heikkilä, L, Reinikainen, A, Katajajuuri, JM, Silvennoinen, K & Hartikainen, H (2016) Elements affecting food waste in the food service sector. *Waste Manag,* 56, 446-53. [http://dx.doi.org/10.1016/j.wasman.2016.06.019] [PMID: 27373724]

Karos, K, Alleva, JM & Peters, ML (2018) Pain, Please: An investigation of sampling bias in pain research. *J Pain,* 19, 787-96. [http://dx.doi.org/10.1016/j.jpain.2018.02.011] [PMID: 29518560]

Liddell, P & Fish, D (2018) *Digital Supply Chain – the hype and the risks,* 8.

Loke, MK & Leung, P (2015) Quantifying food waste in Hawaii's food supply chain. *Waste Manag Res,* 33, 1076-83. [http://dx.doi.org/10.1177/0734242X15607427] [PMID: 26446198]

Martin-Rios, C, Demen-Meier, C, Gössling, S & Cornuz, C (2018) Food waste management innovations in the foodservice industry. *Waste Management,* Elsevier Ltd. 196-206. [http://dx.doi.org/10.1016/j.wasman.2018.07.033]

Mattila, M., Mesiranta, N., Närvänen, E., Koskinen, O., & Sutinen, U.-M. (2019). Dances with potential food waste: Organising temporality in food waste reduction practices. *Time and Society*, 28, 1619-44. [http://dx.doi.org/10.1177/0961463X18784123]

Oelofse, SHH & Nahman, A (2013) Estimating the magnitude of food waste generated in South Africa. *Waste Manag Res,* 31, 80-6. [http://dx.doi.org/10.1177/0734242X12457117] [PMID: 22878934]

Phase, A & Mhetre, N (2018) Using IoT in supply chain management. *International Journal of Engineering and Techniques,* 4, 2395-1303.http://www.ijetjournal.org

Richards, TJ & Hamilton, SF Food waste in the sharing economy. *Food Policy*, Elsevier, 109-23. [http://dx.doi.org/10.1016/j.foodpol.2018.01.008]

Romani, S (2018) *Domestic food practices: A study of food management behaviors and the role of food preparation planning in reducing waste.* Appetite. Elsevier Ltd 215-27. [http://dx.doi.org/10.1016/j.appet.2017.11.093]

Tjahjono, B (2017) 'What does Industry 4. 0 mean to Supply Chain? What does Society to Supply Costing models for capacity optimization in Industry 4. 0 : Trade-off between used capacity and operational efficiency, *Procedia Manufacturing. Elsevier B,* 13, 1175-82. [http://dx.doi.org/10.1016/j.promfg.2]

SUBJECT INDEX

A

Abductive 17, 18
  interpretation 17
  reasoning 18
Activities 27, 31, 32
  digital business 32
  economic 31
  organisation's business 27
Acute asthma 5
  consultations 5
Adoption 51, 107, 113, 114, 115, 116
  factors 107, 113, 114, 115, 116
  of disruptive technology 51
Amazon shopping website 109
Analysis of variance (ANOVA) 135, 141, 142
Application 2, 12, 15, 20, 21, 26, 54, 56, 94,
    100, 101, 111, 123, 131
  mobile 2, 15, 111
  technological 2
Application development 15, 16, 25
  companies 15
  mobile 15, 16
Approaches 2, 9, 19, 29, 34, 51, 54, 55, 64,
    67, 69, 92, 96
  digital 51
  disruptive 19
  innovative governance 67
Artificial intelligence 49, 62, 63, 64, 70, 75,
    76, 87, 89
  adopting 70
  adoption of 64, 70
  algorithms 89
  analytics 49
  implementing 62
  systems 63
  technologies 75, 76, 87, 89
  technology in business innovation 76
  technology in SMEs 76
Assets 33, 35, 38, 39, 65, 66
  digital 38, 39
  essential 66

informational 35
Automating customer conversations 9
Automation, business process 31

B

Behavior 56, 88, 109
  changed consumer 109
  planned 56
Big data 30, 49, 55, 63, 78, 79, 110, 111, 130,
    144
  adoption by SMMEs 110
  analytics 49, 55, 63, 78, 79, 111, 130, 144
  techniques 30
BMI 24, 26, 28, 33
  exploring 28
  processes 24
  technologies 33
  transformations 26
Boosting cost-effectiveness 8
Business 3, 7, 10, 11, 12, 17, 35, 62, 64, 69,
    71, 75, 78, 79, 86, 99, 100, 123
  agility 100
  confidentiality 35
  designs 79
  development agencies 11, 12
  ecosystem 17, 75
  environment 62, 64, 86, 99
  growth 10
  innovation processes 62
  inspirations 3
  intelligence 86, 123
  landscape 71
  network 11, 69
  operations, digital transformation
    revolutionises 75
  problem 10
  sustainability 86
  system 7
  transformation 78
Business innovation 7, 63, 68, 76, 77, 79
  digital 77

www.ingramcontent.com/pod-product-compliance
Lightning Source LLC
Chambersburg PA
CBHW041708210326
41598CB00007B/577